100
Colorful Ripple Stitches
to Crochet

LEONIE MORGAN

St. Martin's Griffin
New York

Library of Congress Cataloging-in-
Publication Data Available Upon Request

ISBN: 978-1-250-04949-0

St. Martin's Griffin books may be purchased
for educational, business, or promotional
use. For information on bulk purchases,
please contact Macmillan Corporate and
Premium Sales Department at 1-800-221-
7945, extension 5442, or write
specialmarkets@macmillan.com

First US Edition: July 2014

QUAR.HRSC

Conceived, designed, and produced by
Quarto Publishing plc
The Old Brewery
6 Blundell Street
London N7 9BH

Project editor: Victoria Lyle
Pattern checker: Therese Chynoweth
Proofreader: Ruth Patrick
Indexer: Helen Snaith
Art director: Caroline Guest
Art editor: Jackie Palmer

Chart illustrations: Kuo Kang Chen
Photography: (swatches) Phil Wilkins;
    (projects) Nicki Dowey
Creative director: Moira Clinch
Publisher: Paul Carslake

Color separation by
PICA Digital Pte Ltd, Singapore
Printed in China by
1010 Printing International Ltd

10 9 8 7 6 5 4 3 2 1

Cover swatch: Rhythm, page 60

Contents

Foreword	6	Hot Star	46	Roman Blinds	80	PROJECT **Afghan:**
About This Book	6	Forest Star	47	Shock Wave	81	**Retro Rose**	**112**
		Arcade	48	Shell Ripple	82	Candy Rose	113
Materials and Notions	8	Marrakesh	49	Summer Ripple	83	Buttons	114
Stitches and Techniques	10	Bright Burst	50	Bobbled Zig-zag	84	Manhattan	115
Reading Patterns and Charts	18	Floral Pop	51	Bloomsbury Bobble	85	Sea Foam	116
Gauge	19	Jasmine	52	PROJECT **Bag: Charleston**	**86**	Ocean Deep	117
Edgings	20	Periwinkle	53	Amalfi	87	Mountain Streams	118
Embellishments	21	Fall Leaves	54	PROJECT **Purse: Jitterbug**	**89**	Sea Shore	119
		Moss Bank	55	Aspen	90	Candy Floss	120
RIPPLE DESIGNS	**22**	Honeydew	56	Plum Strata	91	Ruffle Ripple	121
		Neapolitan	57	Pink Haze	92	Sea of Hearts	122
Rainbow Granny	24	Pink Denim	58	Mulberry Whip	93	Valentine's Day	123
Natural Granny	25	Vibrate	59	Shinto	94	PROJECT **Scarf: Botticelli**	**124**
Bright Waves	26	Rhythm	60	Kyoto	95	Glacier	125
Atlantic Waves	27	70s Groove	61	Confetti	96		
Hill and Valley	28	Syrah	62	Flower Meadow	97		
Topography	29	Merlot	63	Springtime	99	Index	126
Butterfly	30	PROJECT **Pillow:**		Harvest	100	Credits	127
Harmony	31	**San Francisco**	**64**	Bonfire	101	Cascade Yarn List	128
Flames	32	Glade	65	Ocean Swell	102		
Pyrotechnics	33	Berry Ripple	66	Blue Ridge	103		
Mille-Feuille	34	Amethyst	67	Orion's Belt	104		
Tiramisu	35	Lavender Layers	68	Big Dipper	105		
Rainbow Road	36	Sorbet	69	Strawberry Mint	106		
Tuscan Horizon	37	Pastel Posy	70	Raspberry Ripple	107		
Venice	38	Fuchsia Flower	71	Tulips	108		
Florence	39	Pumpkin Patch	72	Easter	109		
Vibrant Vs	40	Halloween	73	Ferris Wheel	110		
Indigo Vs	41	Purple Picots	74	Rosette	111		
Compact Chevrons	42	Shamrock Ripple	75				
Contrast Ripple	43	Red, Stripe, and Blue	76				
PROJECT **Afghan:**		Parisian Bobble	77				
Ice-cream Sundae	**44**	Rock Pool	78				
Coral Reef	45	Metro	79				

Foreword

I've always been a crafty person—"fiddly fingers" is how my mom would describe me. She's the cause of my crochet obsession. The granny blanket she made when I was a child inspired me along the path to becoming a crochet designer.

There isn't a day of the week that I don't pick up a crochet hook. I love turning yarn into beautiful things, like blankets. My home has blankets of all types dotted around and filling cupboards. Many blankets are incomplete or waiting to be joined together.

Among them are ripple blanket projects, which have become the "go-to" projects for chilly evenings. When it's time to shut the curtains and turn the lights on, I drape the unfinished ripple blanket over my lap and leisurely work a few rows.

The brilliance of ripple-stitch patterns is you can use up scraps of yarn from other projects, different textured yarns in all the colors of the rainbow, to crochet a ripple blanket to treasure. Best of all, you have no joining to contend with!

Ripple-stitch patterns aren't used just for blankets either, you can make scarfs, bags, pillows, and clothing. Use the patterns and projects in this book to create whatever you fancy. There is something for everyone within, no matter what your skill level, so grab your hook and dip in.

I hope you enjoy the selection of ripple patterns and I look forward to seeing what your "fiddly fingers" create. Happy Hooking!

Leonie Morgan

About This Book

This book is an eye-catching resource of multiple ripple stitches and projects for you to crochet. As well as the 100 designs, there is information on yarn requirements, crochet tools, and techniques.

Tools and Techniques, pages 8–21

These pages feature everything you need to know to get started, from a summary of the different yarns available to advice on how to read patterns and charts. An illustrated, comprehensive, and concise guide helps you work both the basic crochet stitches and the more advanced stitches used in the book. Finishing techniques—such as edgings and embellishments—are also covered.

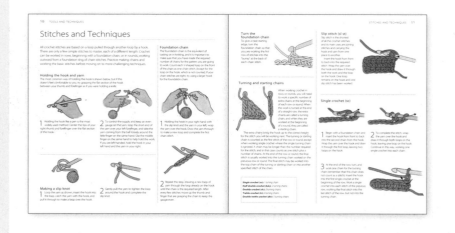

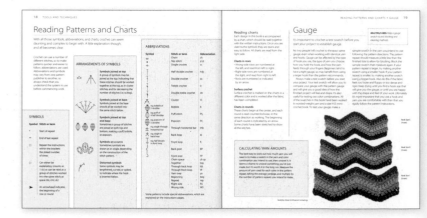

Ripple Designs, pages 22–125

At the heart of this book are the 100 ripple designs: 50 original stitches plus 50 color variations. With written patterns, colored charts, and clear photographs taking you through each one and five fabulous project ideas included, you will want to start crocheting right away.

All the swatches in this book were made with a size H (5 mm) hook and worsted-weight yarn.

A color variation design is included with photograph, color key, and written instructions (where necessary).

Instructions for special stitches used in the pattern are explained.

A key to the colors used in the pattern is included.

A written pattern takes you through the ripple row by row or round by round.

The main design.

Skill level gives a rough guide to difficulty.

A measurement gives you a guide to the size of one pattern repeat.

Photos show the end result.

The main photo shows you how the ripple stitch can be used to make a beautiful project.

Alternating colors in the charts indicate each round/row. A third color would indicate surface crochet.

A full written pattern—including finishing instructions—explains how to make the photographed piece; or you could use all the information on these pages as inspiration for making your own version.

A key to the symbols used in the chart is provided.

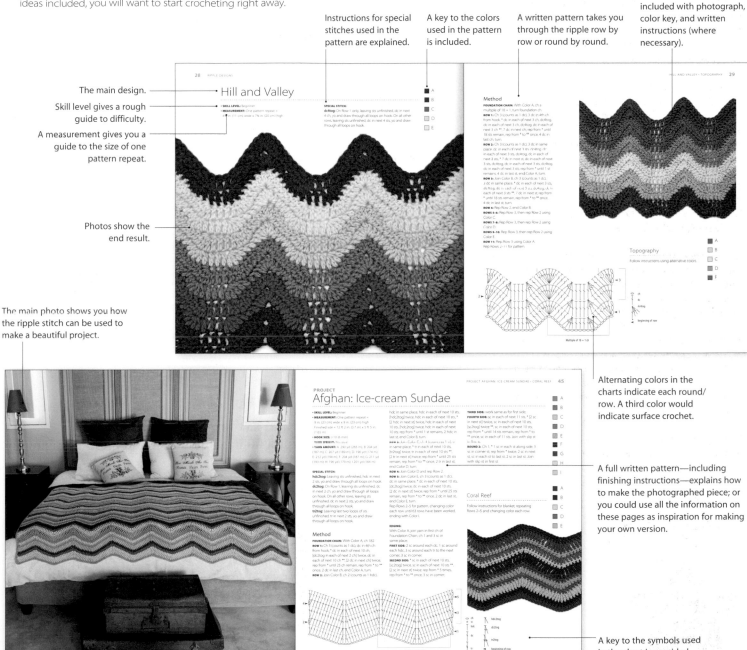

Materials and Notions

When you walk into a yarn store, you'll find yourself bombarded with gorgeous yarns in scrumptious colors, differing weights, and all types of textures. The choice available is exciting and a little perplexing to begin with, and the same can be true for the hooks and accessories. Use the guide below to find out exactly what you need to get started.

Yarns

Suitable yarns for crochet range from very fine cotton to bulky wool and come in a range of different fibers and fiber combinations. As a general rule, yarns that have a smooth texture and a medium or high twist are the easiest to work with. For making afghans, a medium-weight yarn is probably best, as it works up quickly, has good drape and stitch definition, and provides a warm and cozy afghan. All the ripple swatches and projects in this book have been worked in worsted-weight yarn.

Another thing to consider while standing in front of all that yarn is the fiber content and the kind of drape that you would like to achieve in your project.

Before purchasing enough yarn to complete a project, it's a good idea to buy just one ball. Make a test swatch, wash it following the instructions on the ball band, block it to shape, and see whether you are comfortable using the yarn and whether it turns out how you'd intended.

Wool

Wool is an excellent choice for afghans. It is a resilient fiber that feels good to crochet and has great stitch definition. If you are making a project that you would like to hand down to future generations and it is within your budget, wool is the fiber to use. Do find out whether or not the wool can be machine washed.

Acrylic

Acrylic yarn is a perfect choice for beginners and popular with crochet enthusiasts. It's great for practicing stitches and techniques and testing color combinations. Acrylic yarns come in a huge array of colors and it is an affordable choice for your first project. Although acrylic can pill and lose its shape eventually, it does have the benefit of being machine-washable, making it a good choice for items that may require frequent washing.

Combination yarns

A yarn comprised of both wool and synthetic fiber is a dependable choice. Picking something that has a small percentage of synthetic fiber (for example nylon or acrylic) makes a nice yarn to work with and launder while still retaining the advantages of wool.

Cotton and cotton mixes

Cotton can present more of a challenge for beginners. It can be a little stiff to work with, but the stitches are crisp and neat. A cotton mix is usually softer to work with, yet still retains crisp, neat stitch definition. Afghans crocheted with cotton or a cotton mix are durable and cool, so are perfect for summer.

Novelty yarns

Although novelty yarns are tactile and enticing, they are not easy to work with. You can use a splash of novelty yarn to add some interest, but on the whole they are tricky to use and also hide the stitches.

Crochet hooks

Hooks come in different sizes and materials. The material a hook is made from can affect your gauge. To start out, it's best to use aluminum hooks, as they have a pointed head and well-defined throat and work well with most yarns. Bamboo hooks are also pleasing to work with, but can be slippery with some yarns. Plastic hooks can be squeaky with synthetic yarns. You can also purchase hooks with soft-grip or wooden handles, which are great to work with, particularly if crochet becomes an obsession.

What size?

You may find that using the hook size recommended for a particular yarn or pattern isn't satisfactory, and your work may be too tight or too loose. Try different hook sizes until you are happy with the completed swatch. Ultimately, you want to use a hook and yarn weight that you are comfortable with—yarn/hook recommendations are not set in stone.

YARN LABELS: *Not all yarn labels give a recommended hook size. Use the recommended knitting-needle size as a guide, or a hook one or two sizes bigger.*

Size J/
6 mm

Size I/
5.5 mm

Size H/
5 mm

Size G/
4.5 mm

Notions

Although all you need to get started is a hook and some yarn, it's handy to have the following items in your work bag.

Needles

Yarn or tapestry needles are used for sewing seams and weaving in yarn tails. Choose needles with blunt ends to avoid splitting stitches. Yarn needles have different-sized eyes, so choose one that will easily accommodate the weight of yarn you will be using.

Pins

Use rustproof, glass-headed pins for wet and steam blocking.

Stitch markers

Split-ring markers are handy for keeping track of the first stitch of a row, particularly when starting out. Also use them to hold the working loop when you put your work down for the night.

Scissors

Use a pair of small, sharp embroidery scissors.

Ruler and measuring tape

A rigid ruler is best for measuring gauge. A sturdy measuring tape or dressmaking measuring tape with imperial and metric measurements is good for taking larger measurements.

Stitches and Techniques

All crochet stitches are based on a loop pulled through another loop by a hook. There are only a few simple stitches to master, each of a different length. Crochet can be worked in rows, beginning with a foundation chain, or in rounds, working outward from a foundation ring of chain stitches. Practice making chains and working the basic stitches before moving on to more challenging techniques.

Holding the hook and yarn
The most common way of holding the hook is shown below, but if this doesn't feel comfortable to you, try grasping the flat section of the hook between your thumb and forefinger as if you were holding a knife.

1 Holding the hook like a pen is the most widely used method. Center the tips of your right thumb and forefinger over the flat section of the hook.

2 To control the supply and keep an even gauge on the yarn, loop the short end of the yarn over your left forefinger, and take the yarn coming from the ball loosely around the little finger on the same hand. Use the middle finger on the same hand to help hold the work. If you are left-handed, hold the hook in your left hand and the yarn in your right.

Making a slip knot

1 Loop the yarn as shown, insert the hook into the loop, catch the yarn with the hook, and pull it through to make a loop over the hook.

2 Gently pull the yarn to tighten the loop around the hook and complete the slip knot.

Foundation chain
The foundation chain is the equivalent of casting on in knitting, and it is important to make sure that you have made the required number of chains for the pattern you are going to work. Count each V-shaped loop on the front of the chain as one chain stitch, except for the loop on the hook, which is not counted. If your chain stitches are tight, try using a larger hook for the foundation chain.

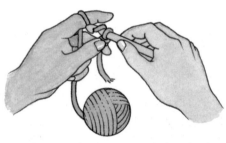

1 Holding the hook in your right hand with the slip knot and the yarn in your left, wrap the yarn over the hook. Draw the yarn through to make a new loop and complete the first chain stitch.

2 Repeat this step, drawing a new loop of yarn through the loop already on the hook until the chain is the required length. After every few stitches move up the thumb and finger that are grasping the chain to keep the gauge even.

Turn the foundation chain

To give a neat starting edge, turn the foundation chain so that you are working the first row of stitches into the "bump" at the back of each chain stitch.

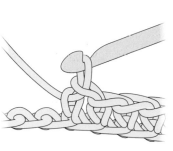

Turning and starting chains

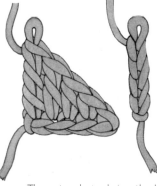

When working crochet in rows or rounds, you will need to work a specific number of extra chains at the beginning of each row or round. When the work is turned at the end of a straight row, the extra chains are called a turning chain, and when they are worked at the beginning of a round, they are called a starting chain.

The extra chains bring the hook up to the correct height for the stitch you will be working next. The turning or starting chain is counted as the first stitch of the row or round, except when working single crochet where the single turning chain is ignored. A chain may be longer than the number required for the stitch, and in that case counts as one stitch plus a number of chains. At the end of the row or round, the final stitch is usually worked into the turning chain worked on the previous row or round. The final stitch may be worked into the top chain of the turning or starting chain or into another specified stitch of the chain.

> **Single crochet (sc):** *1 turning chain*
> **Half double crochet (hdc):** *2 turning chains*
> **Double crochet (dc):** *3 turning chains*
> **Treble crochet (tr):** *4 turning chains*
> **Double treble crochet (dtr):** *5 turning chains*

Slip stitch (sl st)

Slip stitch is the shortest of all the crochet stitches and its main uses are joining stitches and carrying the hook and yarn from one place to another.

Insert the hook from front to back into the required stitch. Wrap the yarn over the hook and draw it through both the work and the loop on the hook. One loop remains on the hook and one slip stitch has been worked.

Single crochet (sc)

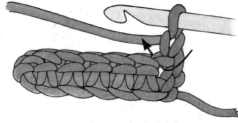

1 Begin with a foundation chain and insert the hook from front to back into the second chain from the hook. Wrap the yarn over the hook and draw it through the first loop, leaving two loops on the hook.

2 To complete the stitch, wrap the yarn over the hook and draw it through both loops on the hook, leaving one loop on the hook. Continue in this way, working one single crochet into each chain.

3 At the end of the row, turn, and work one chain for the turning chain (remember that this chain does not count as a stitch). Insert the hook into the first single crochet at the beginning of the row. Work a single crochet into each stitch of the previous row, working the final stitch into the last stitch of the row, but not into the turning chain.

Half double crochet (hdc)

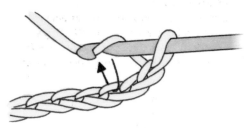

1 Begin with a foundation chain. Wrap the yarn over the hook and insert the hook into the third chain from the hook.

2 Draw the yarn through the chain, leaving three loops. Wrap the yarn over the hook and draw through all three loops on the hook, leaving one loop on the hook.

3 Continue along the row, working one half double crochet into each chain. At the end of the row, work two chains to turn. Miss the first stitch and work a half double crochet into each stitch made on the previous row. At the end of the row, work the last stitch into the top of the turning chain.

Double crochet (dc)

1 Begin with a foundation chain, then wrap the yarn over the hook and insert the hook into the fourth chain from the hook.

2 Draw the yarn through the chain, leaving three loops on the hook. Wrap the yarn again and draw the yarn through the first two loops on the hook, leaving two loops on the hook.

3 Wrap the yarn over the hook, and draw the yarn through the two loops on the hook, leaving one loop on the hook. Repeat along the row. At the end of the row, work three chains to turn. Miss the first stitch and work a double crochet into each stitch. At the end of the row, work the last stitch into the top of the turning chain.

Treble crochet (tr)

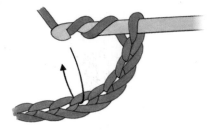

1 Begin with a foundation chain. Wrap the yarn over the hook twice and insert the hook into the fifth chain from the hook.

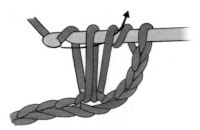

2 Draw the yarn through the chain, leaving four loops on the hook. Wrap the yarn again and draw the yarn through the first two loops on the hook, leaving three loops on the hook.

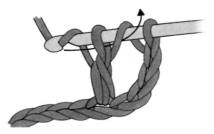

3 Wrap the yarn again and draw through the first two loops on the hook, leaving two loops on the hook.

4 Wrap the yarn again and draw through the two remaining loops, leaving one loop on the hook. Continue along the row, working one treble crochet stitch into each chain. At the end of the row, work four chains to turn. Miss the first stitch and work a treble crochet into each stitch made on the previous row. At the end of the row, work the last stitch into the top of the turning chain.

Working around posts

This technique creates raised stitches by inserting the hook around the post (stem) of the stitch below, from the front or the back.

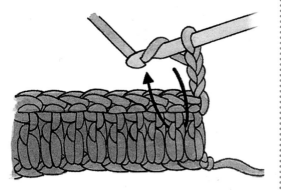

Front post double crochet (FPdc)
Wrap the yarn over the hook from back to front, insert the hook from the front to the back at right of the next stitch, then bring it to the front at the left of the same stitch. Complete the stitch in the usual way.

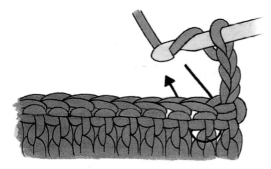

Back post double crochet (BPdc)
Wrap the yarn over the hook, insert the hook from the back to the front at right of the next stitch, then take it back again at the left of the same stitch. Complete the stitch in the usual way.

Working through the horizontal bar

This technique is much the same as working into the front or back loop only. Working into the bar at the back of each stitch raises the front and back loops to add some textured interest.

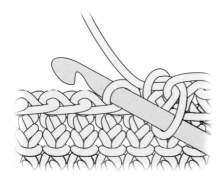

1 Fold stitches forward and insert hook from top to bottom through the horizontal bar or "bump" at the back of the next stitch.

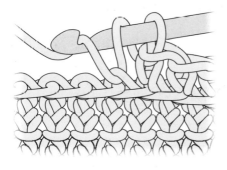

2 Continue working the stitch as normal.

Cluster (Cl)

A cluster is made with a multiple of single, half double, double, or treble crochet stitches. The last loop of each stitch remains on the hook until they are worked together at the end. Count the turning or starting chains as the first stitch.

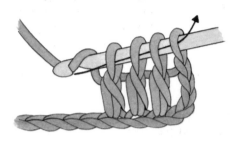

1 To work a cluster of three double-crochet stitches, work the first stitch, omitting the last stage to leave two loops on the hook. Work the second and third stitch in the same way, leaving the last loop of each stitch on the hook. You now have four loops on the hook.

2 Draw the yarn through all four loops to complete the cluster and secure the stitch.

Puff stitch (PS)

A puff stitch is a cluster of half double crochet stitches worked in the same place (the number of stitches may vary). When working a beginning puff stitch, count the turning chain as the first stitch.

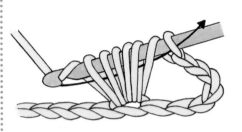

1 Wrap the yarn over the hook, insert the hook where required, and draw a loop through (three loops on the hook). Repeat this step twice more, inserting the hook into the same stitch (seven loops on the hook).

2 Wrap the yarn over the hook and draw it through all seven loops on the hook. Work an extra chain stitch at the top of the puff to complete the stitch.

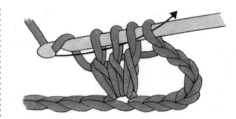

Bobble (B)

A bobble is a group of between three and six double-crochet stitches worked into the same stitch and closed at the top. Bobbles are worked on wrong-side rows and they are usually surrounded by shorter stitches to throw them into high relief. When working bobbles in a contrasting color, use a separate length of yarn to make each bobble, carrying the main yarn under the bobble stitches or across the back of the bobble.

To make a three-stitch bobble, work three double crochet stitches into the same stitch, omitting the last stage of each stitch so the last loop of each one remains on the hook. You now have four loops on the hook. Wrap the yarn over the hook and draw it through the four loops to secure them and complete the bobble.

Popcorn (PC)

A popcorn is a group of double-crochet stitches (the number may vary) sharing the same base stitch, which is folded and closed at the top so the popcorn is raised from the background stitches.

1 To make a popcorn with four stitches, work a group of four double-crochet stitches into the same place.

2 Take the hook out of the working loop and insert it under both loops of the first double crochet in the group. Pick up the working loop with the hook and draw it through to fold the group of stitches and close it at the top.

Spike stitch (Ss)

Spike stitches are made by inserting the hook one or more rows below the previous row, either directly below the next stitch or to the left or right.

To work a single-crochet spike stitch, insert the hook as directed by the pattern, wrap the yarn over the hook and draw through, lengthen the loop to the height of the working row, then complete the stitch.

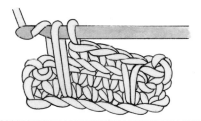

Decreases

One or two stitches can be decreased by working two or three incomplete stitches together, and the method is the same for single, half double, double, and treble crochet stitches.

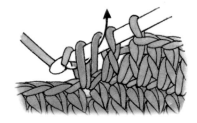

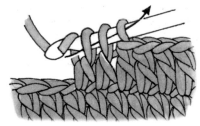

1 Leave the first stitch incomplete so there are two loops on the hook, then work another incomplete stitch so you have three loops on the hook.

2 Wrap the yarn and draw through all three loops to finish the decrease. Two stitches can be decreased in the same way by working three stitches together. When working in double crochet, this decrease is called dc3tog.

Bead stitch

A bead stitch is made by working a cluster of hdc around the previous stitch.

1 Wrap the yarn over the hook, insert the hook from right to left around the post of the previous double crochet, wrap the yarn over the hook and draw up a loop. Repeat twice more until seven loops are on the hook.

2 Wrap the yarn over the hook and draw through all seven loops on hook.

Working in rounds

Crochet worked in rounds is worked outward from a central ring of chains, called a Foundation Ring, or from a Magic Ring (see right).

Making a Foundation Ring

Work a short length of foundation chain as specified in the pattern. Join the chains into a ring by working a slip stitch into the first stitch of the foundation chain.

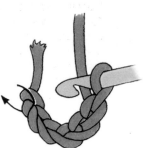

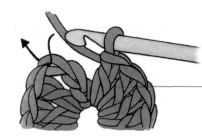

Working into the ring

1 Work the number of starting chains specified in the pattern—three chains are shown here (counting as one double-crochet stitch). Inserting the hook into the space at the center of the ring each time, work the number of stitches specified in the pattern.

2 Count the stitches at the end of the round to check that you have worked the correct number. Join the first and last stitches of the round together by working a slip stitch into the top (or other specified stitch) of the starting chain.

Finishing off the final round—an alternative to slip stitch join

1 Cut the yarn, leaving a tail of about 4 in. (10 cm), and draw it through the last stitch. With right side facing, thread the tail in a yarn needle and take it under both loops of the stitch next to the starting chain.

2 Insert the needle into the center of the last stitch of the round. On the wrong side, pull the needle through to complete the stitch, adjust the length of the stitch to close the round, then weave in the tail on the wrong side and trim.

Making a Magic Ring

A Magic Ring can be used in place of a Foundation Ring for crocheting in the round. The benefit of this method is that after pulling the yarn tail to draw the stitches together there is no hole at the center of your work.

1 Wind the yarn around your finger once, leaving the yarn tail on the left and the working yarn on the right.

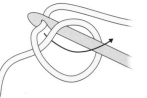

2 Insert your hook under the strands of the ring and draw through a loop of the working yarn.

3 Now work the number of starting chains required in the pattern.

4 Continue in the same manner as for working into a Foundation Ring.

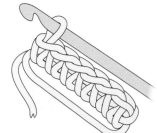

5 When the first round is complete, pull tightly on the yarn tail to close the Magic Ring.

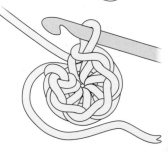

Joining a new color when working in the round

When the pattern states "Join Color B," this is done in the same place the old yarn ended, usually at the start of a round. To join a new color, insert the hook in the work as instructed, draw up a loop of the new color leaving a tail about 4 in. (10 cm) long, and chain 1. Continue with new yarn.

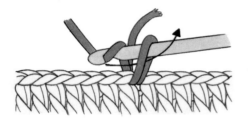

Changing colors at the start or middle of a row

When working the last stitch of the old color, leave the stitch incomplete, wrap the new color around the hook, and finish the stitch.

1 Draw the new color through the last two loops of the stitch.

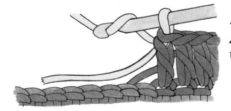

2 Continue working in the new color.

Weaving in ends

For crochet worked in rows, sew in ends diagonally on the wrong side. For crochet worked in the round, sew in ends under stitches for a couple of inches. If the pattern doesn't allow this, sew under a few stitches, then up through the back of a stitch, and under a few more stitches on the next row.

Surface crochet

Surface crochet is worked onto the crochet block when it is complete; the stitches used are usually chain stitch or single crochet and can be used to "draw" lines, swirls, and letters. You can also work other stitches on the surface of the fabric, for instance, single crochet or double crochet. Work around the posts of stitches or through the gaps between stitches.

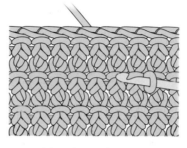

1 Holding the working yarn at the back of your work at all times, insert the hook from front to back through the fabric in a space between two stitches and pull through a loop.

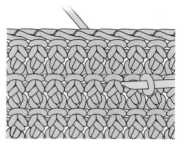

2 Insert hook from front to back in space between next two stitches.

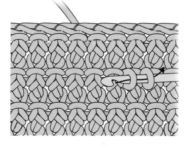

3 Pull up a loop.

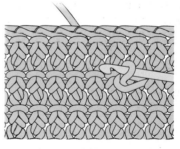

4 Pull loop through the loop on the hook to make a chain stitch.

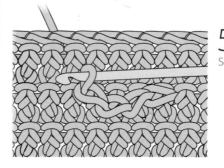

5 Continue in this way, working chain stitches to form a pattern. Secure yarn ends.

Reading Patterns and Charts

With all those symbols, abbreviations, and charts, crochet can seem daunting and complex to begin with. A little explanation though, and all becomes clear.

Crochet can use a number of different stitches, so to make patterns quicker and easier to follow, abbreviations are used. Abbreviations and symbols may vary from one pattern publisher to another, so always check that you understand the system in use before commencing work.

SYMBOLS

Symbol	Stitch or term
*	Start of repeat
**	End of last repeat
[ ]	Repeat the instructions within the brackets the stated number of times
( )	Can either be explanatory (counts as 1 dc) or can be read as a group of stitches worked into the same stitch or space (dc, ch2, dc)
➤	An arrowhead indicates the beginning of a row or round

ARRANGEMENTS OF SYMBOLS

Symbols joined at top
A group of symbols may be joined at the top, indicating that these stitches should be worked together at the top, as in cluster stitches, and for decreasing the number of stitches (i.e. sc3tog).

Symbols joined at base
Symbols joined at the base should all be worked into the same stitch below.

Symbols joined at top and base
Sometimes a group of stitches are joined at both top and bottom, making a puff, bobble, or popcorn.

Symbols on a curve
Sometimes symbols are drawn at an angle, depending on the construction of the stitch pattern.

Distorted symbols
Some symbols may be lengthened, curved, or spiked, to indicate where the hook is inserted below.

ABBREVIATIONS

Symbol	Stitch or term	Abbreviation
○	Chain	ch
●	Slip stitch	sl st
┼	Single crochet	sc
⊤	Half double crochet	hdc
⊦	Double crochet	dc
⊨	Treble crochet	tr
⊧	Double treble crochet	dtr
丰	Cluster	Cl
e.g. bobble of 5 doubles	Bobble	B
e.g. puff of 4 half doubles	Puff stitch	PS
e.g. popcorn of 5 doubles	Popcorn	PC
e.g. single through horizontal bar	Through horizontal bar	thb
e.g. single in back loop	Back loop	bl
e.g. half double in front loop	Front loop	fl
	Back post	BP
	Front post	FP
	Chain space	ch sp
	Together	tog
	Through back loop	tbl
	Through front loop	tfl
	Yarn over	yo
	Beginning	beg
	Repeat	rep
	Right side	RS
	Wrong side	WS

Some patterns include special abbreviations, which are explained on the instructions pages.

Reading charts

Each design in this book is accompanied by a chart, which should be read together with the written instructions. Once you are used to the symbols they are quick and easy to follow. All charts are read from the right side.

Charts in rows

- Wrong-side rows are numbered at the left, and read from left to right.
- Right-side rows are numbered at the right, and read from right to left.
- Rows are numbered or indicated by an arrow.

Surface crochet

Surface crochet is marked on the charts in a different color and is worked after the fabric has been completed.

Charts in rounds

These charts begin at the center, and each round is read counterclockwise, in the same direction as working. The beginning of each round is indicated by an arrow. Some charts have been stretched to show all the stitches.

Gauge

It's important to crochet a test swatch before you start your project to establish gauge.

No two people will crochet to the exact same gauge, even when working with identical yarn and hooks. Gauge can be affected by the type of hook you use, the type of yarn you choose, how you hold the hook, and how the yarn feeds through your fingers. Beginners tend to have a tight gauge, so may benefit from using a larger hook than the pattern recommends.

Always make a test swatch before you start your project. Your test swatch will allow you to compare your gauge with the pattern gauge and will give you a good idea of how the finished project will feel and drape. It's also useful for testing out color combinations. All of the swatches in this book have been worked in worsted-weight yarn and a size H (5 mm) crochet hook. To test your gauge, make a

sample swatch in the yarn you intend to use following the pattern directions. The pattern repeat should measure a little less than the finished size to allow for blocking. Block the sample swatch then measure again. If your pattern repeat is larger, try making another swatch using a smaller hook. If your pattern repeat is smaller, try making another swatch using a bigger hook. Also do this if the fabric feels too loose and floppy or too dense and rigid. Keep trying until you find a hook size that will give you the gauge, or until you are happy with the drape and feel of your work. Ultimately it's more important that you use a hook and yarn you are comfortable with than that you rigidly follow the pattern instructions.

MULTIPLE USES: *Keep a gauge swatch to test blocking and cleaning methods.*

CALCULATING YARN AMOUNTS

The best way to work out how much yarn you will need is to make a swatch in the yarn and color combination you intend to use, then unravel it. It seems a shame to unravel something you've just made, but it's worth it in the long run. Measure the amount of yarn used for each color in the pattern repeat, taking the average yardage, and multiply by the number of pattern repeats you intend to make.

Hook Size G (4 mm)

Hook Size H (5 mm)

Hook Size J (6 mm)

Swatches shown at 40 percent actual size

Edgings

You may wish to work a simple edging around your finished ripple afghan to neaten the edges. Use a hook a size or two smaller than the one you used for the main project.

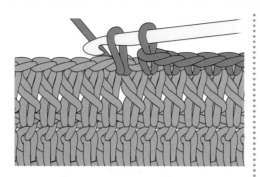

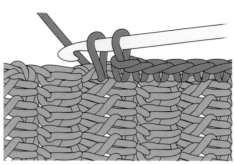

Working across the top or bottom edge

Work 1 sc into each stitch. To work into the ripple points and valleys, follow the increases and decreases as set in the ripple pattern. If you find the edging is too wavy or too taut after a few points and valleys have been worked, it will probably get worse as you continue around. Take time at this point to pull out the first row or round and redo it using more or less stitches.

Working along sides of row ends

When working on a side edge insert the hook under two threads of the first (or last) stitch of each row. Place the stitches an even distance apart along the edge. Try a short length to test the number of stitches required for a flat result. As a guide:

ROWS OF SC: 1 sc in side edge of each row.
ROWS OF HDC: 3 sc in side edge of every two rows.
ROWS OF DC: 2 sc in side edge of every row.
ROWS OF TR: 3 sc in side edge of each row.

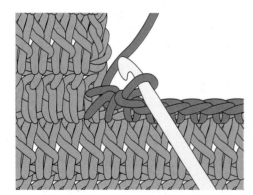

Inward corner

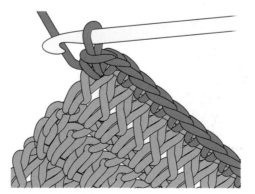

Outer corner

Working around corners

You'll need to add a couple of stitches at each corner to allow the edging to turn without distorting your work. As a guide, outer corners are normally turned by working 3 sc (or sc, hdc, sc) into the corner. For inward corners you'll need to decrease. As a guide, work a sc3tog as pictured left.

Embellishments

You can embellish and personalize your crochet fabric with appliqué, embroidery, buttons, ribbons, and beads. Dig out your sewing box, and let your imagination run free!

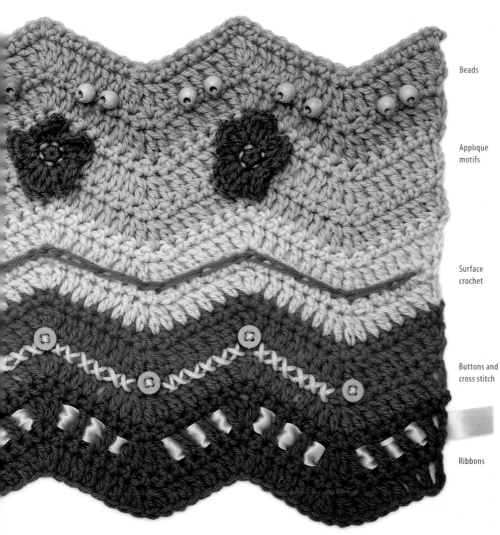

Beads

Appliqué motifs

Surface crochet

Buttons and cross stitch

Ribbons

Swatch shown at 50 percent actual size

Embroidery

Use simple embroidery stitches such as backstitch, running stitch, and lazy daisy to create your own designs. Try embroidering a name or phrase as a personal touch. For embroidery work it's best to use a blunt wool needle to avoid damaging the stitches by splitting the threads.

Beads

Sew beads or sequins to the finished block to add a splash of sparkle. Use sewing thread and attach securely. Or, you can thread the yarn with beads or sequins and use them randomly on a wrong-side row as pictured.

Appliqué motifs

Sewing crochet motifs onto crochet fabric is another great way to embellish your work. Motifs worked in a yarn with different fiber content can add interest.

Surface crochet

Working surface crochet onto the fabric is another way of embroidering and embellishing your work. Work simple chain stitches to create swirly lines or letters.

Buttons

Attach simple, shaped, or vintage buttons to the fabric. Use buttons to create patterns, or just add them at every point of the ripple stitch.

Ribbons

Weave ribbons through larger stitches and secure at the back of the work to add some shimmer.

Ripple Designs

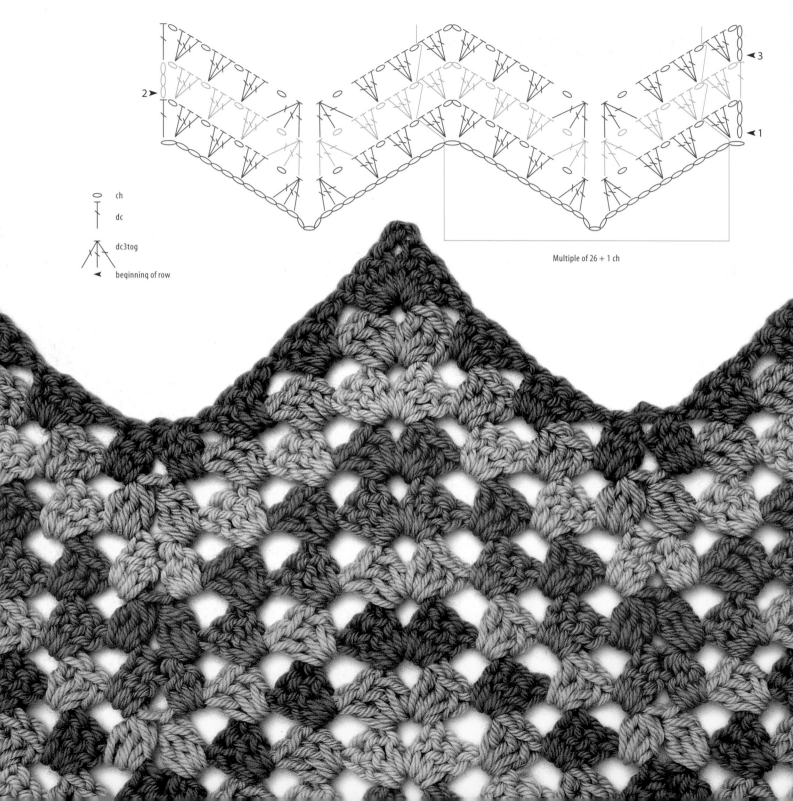

2 ►

◄ 3

◄ 1

ch
dc
dc3tog
beqinninq of row

Multiple of 26 + 1 ch

Rainbow Granny

- **SKILL LEVEL:** Beginner
- **MEASUREMENT:** One pattern repeat =
  5 in. (13 cm) wide x 7 in. (18 cm) high

SPECIAL STITCH:

dc3tog: On Row 1, leaving sts unfinished,
dc in next 3 ch, yo and draw through all loops
on hook.
On all other rows, leaving sts unfinished, 3 dc in
(next dc, ch-1 sp, next dc), yo and draw through
all loops on hook.

Method

FOUNDATION CHAIN: With Color A, ch a multiple
of 26 + 1, turn foundation ch.

ROW 1: Ch 4 (counts as 1 dc, ch 1), 3 dc in same
ch, ch 1, * [skip 2 ch, 3 dc in next ch, ch 1] twice,
skip 2 ch, dc3tog in next 3 ch, skip 3 ch, dc3tog
in next 3 ch, [ch 1, skip 2 ch, 3 dc in next ch] twice,
ch 1, skip 2 ch **, (3 dc, ch 2, 3 dc) in next ch; rep
from * until 26 ch remain, rep from * to ** once,
dc in last ch, end Color A, turn.

ROW 2: Join Color B, ch 4 (counts as 1 dc, ch 1),
[3 dc in ch-sp, ch 1] 3 times, [dc3tog] twice,
[ch 1, 3 dc in ch-sp] twice, ch 1, * (3 dc, ch 2,
3 dc) in ch-2 sp, [ch 1, 3 dc in ch-sp] twice,
ch 1, [dc3tog] twice, [ch 1, 3 dc in ch-sp] twice;
rep from * until 1 dc group remains, 3 dc in last
ch-sp, ch 1, dc in last st, end Color B, turn.

ROW 3: Join Color C, ch 4 (counts as 1 dc, ch 1),
[3 dc in ch-sp, ch 1] 3 times, [dc3tog] twice,
[ch 1, 3 dc in ch-sp] twice, ch 1, * (3 dc, ch 2,
3 dc) in ch-2 sp, [ch 1, 3 dc in ch-sp] twice,
ch 1, [dc3tog] twice, [ch 1, 3 dc in ch-sp] twice;
rep from * until 1 dc group remains, 3 dc in last
ch-sp, ch 1, dc in last st, end Color C, turn.

ROW 4: Rep Row 2 using Color D.

ROW 5: Rep Row 3 using Color E.

ROW 6: Rep Row 2 using Color F.

ROW 7: Rep Row 3 using Color A.

Rep Rows 2–7 for pattern.

■ A
□ B
□ C
■ D
□ E
■ F

Natural Granny

□ A
■ B
□ C

Follow instructions using alternative colors:

ROWS 1–2: Color A
ROWS 3–4: Color B
ROWS 5–6: Color C
ROW 7: Color A
Rep Rows 2–7 for pattern

Bright Waves

- **SKILL LEVEL:** Beginner
- **MEASUREMENT:** One pattern repeat =
  6 in. (15 cm) wide x 12¾ in. (32.5 cm) high

Method

FOUNDATION CHAIN: With Color A, ch a multiple of 18 + 3, turn foundation ch.

ROW 1: Ch 1, sc in 2nd ch from hook, * sc in each of next 2 ch, hdc in each of next 3 ch, dc in each of next 3 ch, tr in each of next 3 ch, dc in each of next 3 ch, hdc in each of next 3 ch, sc in next ch; rep from * until 2 ch remain, sc in each of last 2 ch, end Color A, turn.

ROW 2: Join Color B, ch 4 (counts as 1 tr), tr in next st, * tr in next st, dc in each of next 3 sts, hdc in each of next 3 sts, sc in each of next 3 sts, hdc in each of next 3 sts, dc in each of next 3 sts, tr in each of next 2 sts; rep from * until 1 st remains, tr in last st, end Color B, turn.

ROW 3: Join Color C, ch 1 and sc in same place, * sc in each of next 2 sts, hdc in each of next 3 sts, dc in each of next 3 sts, tr in each of next 3 sts, dc in each of next 3 sts, hdc in each of next 3 sts, sc in next st; rep from * until 2 sts remain, sc in each of last 2 sts, end Color C, turn.

ROW 4: Rep Row 2 using Color D.
ROW 5: Rep Row 3 using Color E.
ROW 6: Rep Row 2 using Color A.
ROW 7: Rep Row 3 using Color B.
ROW 8: Rep Row 2 using Color C.
ROW 9: Rep Row 3 using Color D.
ROW 10: Rep Row 2 using Color E.
ROW 11: Rep Row 3 using Color A.
Rep Rows 2–11 for pattern.

ch · ○
sc · +
hdc · ┬
dc · ┬/
tr · ┬//
beginning of row · ◄

Atlantic Waves

· **MEASUREMENT:** One pattern repeat = 6 in. (15 cm) wide x 12¾ in. (32.5 cm) high

Follow instructions using alternative colors.

ROW 1: Color A
ROW 2: Color B
ROW 3: Color C
ROW 4: Color D
ROW 5: Color E
ROW 6: Color F
ROW 7: Rep Row 3 using Color A
Rep Rows 2–7 for pattern.

☐ A
☐ B
☐ C
☐ D
☐ E
☐ F

Multiple of 18 + 3 ch

Hill and Valley

- **SKILL LEVEL:** Beginner
- **MEASUREMENT:** One pattern repeat =
  4¼ in. (11 cm) wide x 7¾ in. (20 cm) high

SPECIAL STITCH:

dc4tog: On Row 1 only, leaving sts unfinished, dc in next 4 ch, yo and draw through all loops on hook. On all other rows, leaving sts unfinished, dc in next 4 sts, yo and draw through all loops on hook.

■ A
■ B
■ C
□ D
□ E

Method

FOUNDATION CHAIN: With Color A, ch a multiple of 18 + 1, turn foundation ch.

ROW 1: Ch 3 (counts as 1 dc), 3 dc in 4th ch from hook, * dc in each of next 3 ch, dc4tog, dc in each of next 3 ch, dc4tog, dc in each of next 3 ch **, 7 dc in next ch; rep from * until 18 sts remain, rep from * to ** once, 4 dc in last ch, turn.

ROW 2: Ch 3 (counts as 1 dc), 3 dc in same place, dc in each of next 3 sts, dc4tog, dc in each of next 3 sts, dc4tog, dc in each of next 3 sts, * 7 dc in next st, dc in each of next 3 sts, dc4tog, dc in each of next 3 sts, dc4tog, dc in each of next 3 sts; rep from * until 1 st remains, 4 dc in last st, end Color A, turn.

ROW 3: Join Color B, ch 3 (counts as 1 dc), 3 dc in same place, * dc in each of next 3 sts, dc4tog, dc in each of next 3 sts, dc4tog, dc in each of next 3 sts **, 7 dc in next st; rep from * until 18 sts remain, rep from * to ** once, 4 dc in last st, turn.

ROW 4: Rep Row 2, end Color B.

ROWS 5–6: Rep Row 3, then rep Row 2 using Color C.

ROWS 7–8: Rep Row 3, then rep Row 2 using Color D.

ROWS 9–10: Rep Row 3, then rep Row 2 using Color E.

ROW 11: Rep Row 3 using Color A.

Rep Rows 2–11 for pattern.

Topography

Follow instructions using alternative colors.

	A
	B
	C
	D
	E

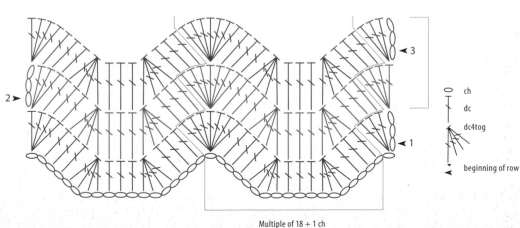

ch

dc

dc4tog

beginning of row

Multiple of 18 + 1 ch

Butterfly

- **SKILL LEVEL:** Beginner
- **MEASUREMENT:** One pattern repeat =
  5 in. (13 cm) wide x 7½ in. (19 cm) high

SPECIAL STITCH:

dc5tog: Leaving sts unfinished, [dc in next st
or ch, skip 1] 4 times, dc in next st or ch,
yo and draw through all loops on hook.

Method

FOUNDATION CHAIN: With Color A, ch a multiple of 32 + 1, turn foundation ch.

ROW 1: Ch 4 (counts as 1 dc, ch 1), (dc, ch 1, dc) in 5th ch from hook, * [ch 1, skip 1 ch, dc in next ch] 5 times, ch 1, dc5tog, [ch 1, skip 1 ch, dc in next ch] 5 times, ch 1 **, ([dc, ch 1] 4 times, dc) in next ch; rep from * until 32 ch remain, rep from * to ** once, (dc, ch 1, dc, ch 1, dc) in last ch, turn.

ROW 2: Ch 4 (counts as 1 dc, ch 1), (dc, ch 1, dc) in same place, [ch 1, skip ch-1 sp, dc in next st] 5 times, ch 1, dc5tog, [ch 1, skip ch-1 sp, dc in next st] 5 times, ch 1, * ([dc, ch 1] 4 times, dc) in next st, [ch 1, skip ch-1 sp, dc in next st] 5 times, ch 1, dc5tog, [ch 1, skip ch-1 sp, dc in next st] 5 times, ch 1; rep from * until 1 st remains, (dc, ch 1, dc, ch 1, dc) in last st, end Color A, turn.

ROW 3: Join Color B, ch 4 (counts as 1 dc, ch 1), (dc, ch 1, dc) in same place, * [ch 1, skip ch-1 sp, dc in next st] 5 times, ch 1, dc5tog, [ch 1, skip ch-1 sp, dc in next st] 5 times, ch 1, * ([dc, ch 1] 4 times, dc) in next st; rep from * until 16 dc remain, rep from * to ** once, (dc, ch 1, dc, ch 1, dc) in last st, turn.

Rep Rows 2 and 3 for pattern. Work 2 rows in each color.

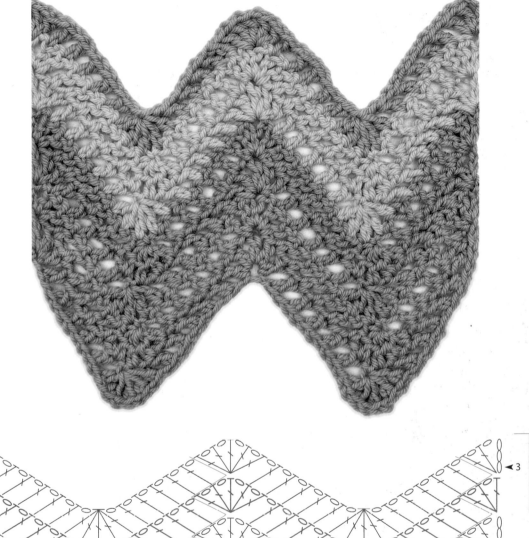

Harmony

Follow instructions using alternative colors.

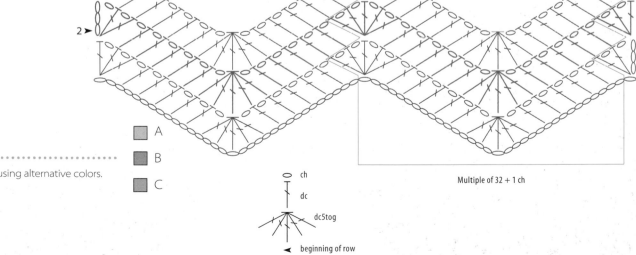

A

B

C

○ ch

| dc

dc5tog

◄ beginning of row

Multiple of 32 + 1 ch

Flames

- **SKILL LEVEL:** Beginner
- **MEASUREMENT:** One pattern repeat =
  4 in. (10 cm) wide x 5 in. (13 cm) high

SPECIAL STITCH:

sc2tog: Leaving sts unfinished, sc in next 2 sts, yo and draw through all loops on hook.

■ A
■ B
□ C
■ D
□ E
□ F

Method

FOUNDATION CHAIN: With Color A, ch a multiple of 19 + 1, turn foundation ch.

ROW 1: Ch 3 (counts as 1 dc), 2 dc in 4th ch from hook, dc in each of next 3 ch, hdc in each of next 2 ch, [sc2tog] 4 times, hdc in each of next 2 ch, dc in each of next 3 ch **, (2 dc, tr, 2 dc) in next ch; rep from * until 19 ch remain, rep from * to ** once, 3 dc in last ch, end Color A, do not turn.

ROW 2: Join Color B in top of ch-3 at the beginning of last row, ch 3 (counts as 1 dc), 2 dc in same place, * dc in each of next 3 sts, hdc in each of next 2 sts, [sc2tog] 4 times, hdc in each of next 2 sts, dc in each of next 3 sts **, (2 dc, tr, 2 dc) in next st; rep from * until 19 sts remain, rep from * to ** once, 3 dc in last st, end Color B, do not turn.

ROW 3: Rep Row 2 using Color C.
ROW 4: Rep Row 2 using Color D.
ROW 5: Rep Row 2 using Color E.
ROW 6: Rep Row 2 using Color F.
ROW 7: Rep Row 2 using Color A.
Rep Rows 2–7 for pattern.

Pyrotechnics

• **MEASUREMENT:** One pattern repeat = 6 in. (15 cm) wide x 12¾ in. (32.5 cm) high

Follow instructions using alternative colors:

ROW 1: Color A	**ROW 6:** Color F	**ROW 11:** Color A
ROW 2: Color B	**ROW 7:** Color E	Rep Rows 2–11 for
ROW 3: Color C	**ROW 8:** Color D	pattern.
ROW 4: Color D	**ROW 9:** Color C	
ROW 5: Color E	**ROW 10:** Color B	

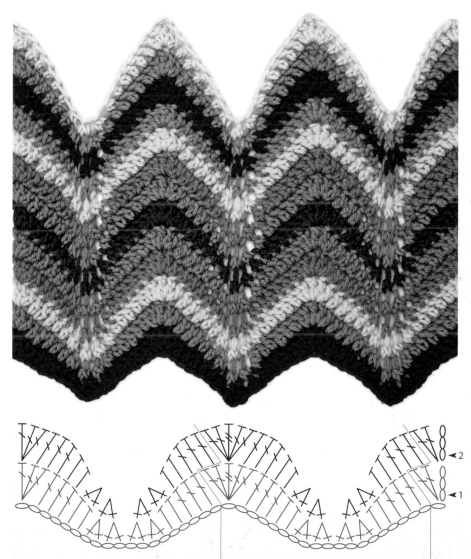

○ ch
+ sc
⊤ hdc
† dc
‡ tr
⋀ sc2tog
◄ beginning of row

Multiple of 19 + 1 ch

Mille-Feuille

- **SKILL LEVEL:** Beginner
- **MEASUREMENT:** One pattern repeat =
  5½ in. (14 cm) wide x 5 in. (13 cm) high

SPECIAL STITCH:

hdc2tog: On Row 1 only, leaving sts unfinished, hdc in next 2 ch, yo and draw through all loops on hook. On all other rows, leaving sts unfinished, hdc in next 2 sts, yo and draw through all loops on hook.

A
B
C
D
E
F
G

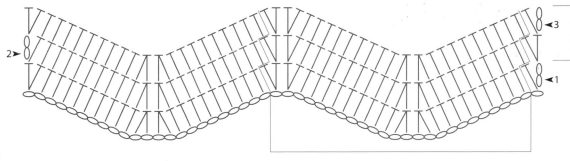

ch

hdc

hdc2tog

beginning of row

Multiple of 24 ch

Method

FOUNDATION CHAIN: With Color A, ch a multiple of 24, turn foundation ch.

ROW 1: Ch 2 (counts as 1 hdc), hdc in 3rd ch from hook, * hdc in each of next 9 ch, [hdc2tog] twice, hdc in each of next 9 ch **, [2 hdc in next ch] twice; rep from * until 23 ch remain, rep from * to ** once, 2 hdc in last ch, end Color A, turn.

ROW 2: Join Color B, ch 2 (counts as 1 hdc), hdc in same place, hdc in each of next 9 sts, [hdc2tog] twice, hdc in each of next 9 sts, * [2 hdc in next st] twice, hdc in each of next 9 sts, [hdc2tog] twice, hdc in each of next 9 sts; rep from * until 1 st remains, 2 hdc in last st, end Color B, turn.

ROW 3: Join Color C, ch 2 (counts as 1 hdc), hdc in same place, * hdc in each of next 9 sts, [hdc2tog] twice, hdc in each of next 9 sts **, [2 hdc in next st] twice; rep from * until 23 sts remain, rep from * to ** once, 2 hdc in last st, end Color C, turn.

ROW 4: Rep Row 2 using Color D.

ROW 5: Rep Row 3 using Color E.

ROW 6: Rep Row 2 using Color F.

ROW 7: Rep Row 3 using Color G.

ROW 8: Rep Row 2 using Color A.

Rep Rows 2–8 for pattern, changing color each row.

Tiramisu

Follow instructions using alternative colors.

ROWS 1–2: Color A
ROWS 3–4: Color B
ROWS 5–6: Color C
ROWS 7–8: Color D
ROW 9: Color A
Rep Rows 2–9 for pattern.

A

B

C

D

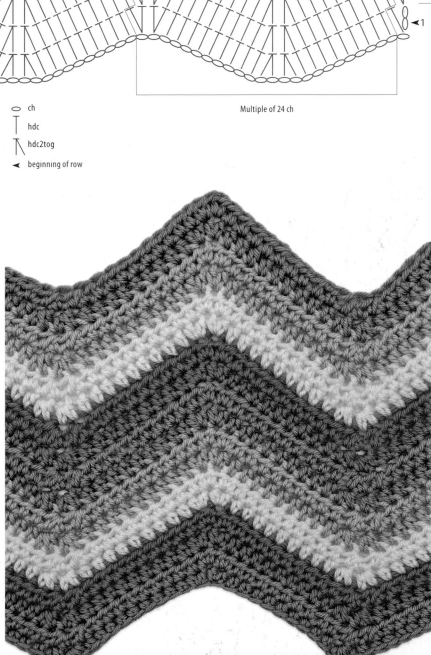

Rainbow Road

- **SKILL LEVEL:** Beginner
- **MEASUREMENT:** One pattern repeat =
  3½ in. (9 cm) wide x 5½ in. (14 cm) high

SPECIAL STITCH:

dc2tog: On Row 1 only, leaving sts unfinished, dc in next ch, skip 3 ch, dc in next ch, yo and draw through all loops on hook.

On all other rows, leaving sts unfinished, dc in next st, skip 1 st, dc in next st, yo and draw through all loops on hook.

A

B

C

D

E

F

G

Method

FOUNDATION CHAIN: With Color A, ch a multiple of 14 + 1, turn foundation ch.

ROW 1: Ch 3 (counts as 1 dc), dc in 4th ch from hook, * dc in each of next 4 ch, dc2tog, dc in each of next 4 ch **, (dc, ch 1, dc) in next ch; rep from * until 14 ch remain, rep from * to **, 2 dc in last ch, end Color A, turn.

ROW 2: Join Color B, ch 3 (counts as 1 dc), dc in same place, dc in each of next 4 sts, dc2tog, dc in each of next 4 sts, * (dc, ch 1, dc) in ch-1 sp, dc in each of next 4 sts, dc2tog, dc in each of next 4 sts; rep from * until 1 st remains, 2 dc in last st, end Color B, turn.

ROW 3: Join Color C, ch 3 (counts as 1 dc), dc in same place, * dc in each of next 4 sts, dc2tog, dc in each of next 4 sts **, (dc, ch 1, dc) in ch-1 sp; rep from * until 12 sts remain, rep from * to ** once, 2 dc in last st, end Color C, turn.

ROW 4: Rep Row 2 using Color D.

ROW 5: Rep Row 3 using Color E.

ROW 6: Rep Row 2 using Color F.

ROW 7: Rep Row 2 using Color G.

ROW 8: Rep Row 3 using Color A.

Rep Rows 2–8 for pattern.

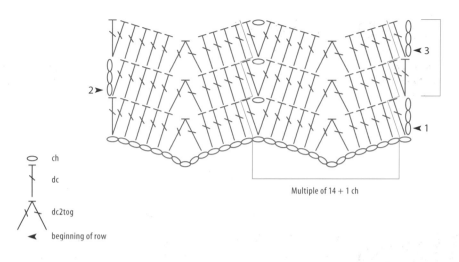

ch

dc

dc2tog

beginning of row

Multiple of 14 + 1 ch

Tuscan Horizon

Follow instructions using alternative colors.

ROWS 1–2: Color A

ROWS 3–4: Color B

ROWS 5–6: Color C

ROWS 7–8: Color D

ROWS 9–10: Color E

ROW 11: Color A

Rep Rows 2–11 for pattern.

A

B

C

D

E

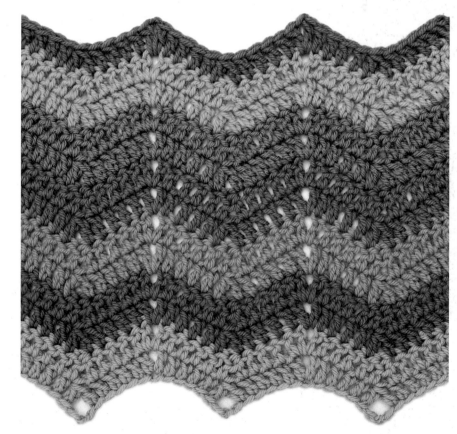

Venice

- **SKILL LEVEL:** Beginner
- **MEASUREMENT:** One pattern repeat = 3½ in. (9 cm) wide x 5½ in. (14 cm) high

A
B
C
D
E
F

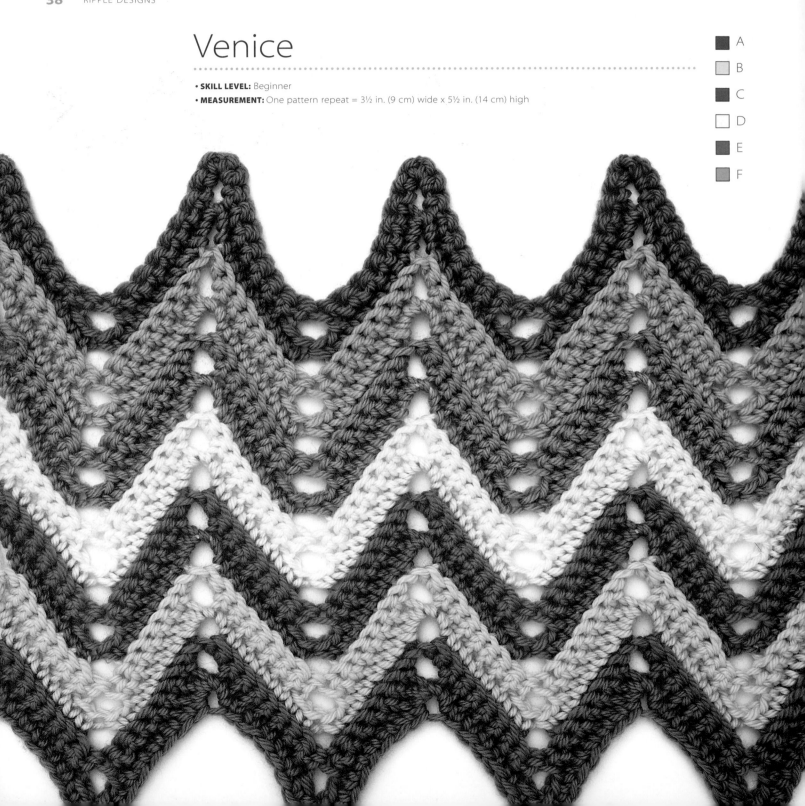

Method

FOUNDATION CHAIN: With Color A, ch a multiple of 19 + 1, turn foundation ch.

ROW 1: Ch 1, 3 sc in 2nd ch from hook, * sc in next 7 ch, skip next 4 ch, sc in next 7 ch **, 5 sc in next ch; rep from * until 19 ch remain, rep from * to ** once, 3 sc in last ch, turn.

ROW 2: Ch 1, working in back loop only 3 sc in same place, sc tbl in next 7 sts, skip next 4 sts, sc tbl in next 7 sts, * 5 sc tbl in next st, sc tbl in next 7 sts, skip next 4 sts, sc tbl in next 7 sts; rep from * until 1 st remains, 3 sc tbl in last st, end Color A, turn.

ROW 3: Join Color B, ch 1, 3 sc tbl in same place, * sc tbl in next 7 sts, skip next 4 sts, sc tbl in next 7 sts **, 5 sc tbl in next st; rep from * until 19 sts remain, rep from * to ** once, 3 sc tbl in last st, turn.

ROW 4: Rep Row 2 using Color B.

ROWS 5–6: Rep Row 3, then Row 2 using Color C.

ROWS 7–8: Rep Rows 5–6 using Color D.

ROWS 9–10: Rep Rows 5–6 using Color E.

ROWS 11–12: Rep Rows 5–6 using Color F.

ROW 13: Rep Row 3 using Color A.

Rep Rows 2–13 for pattern.

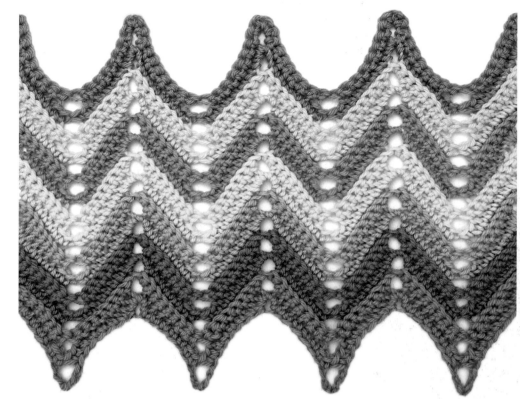

Florence

Follow instructions using alternative colors.

A
B
C
D
E
F

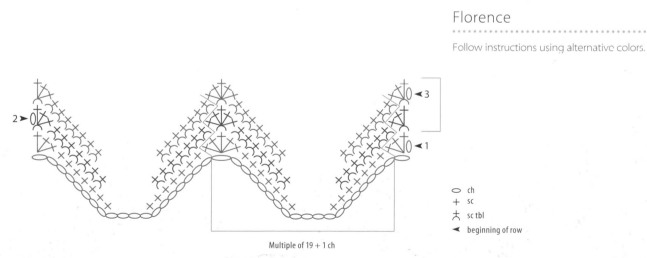

○ ch
+ sc
大 sc tbl
◄ beginning of row

Multiple of 19 + 1 ch

Vibrant Vs

A
B
C
D
E

· **SKILL LEVEL:** Beginner
· **MEASUREMENT:** One pattern repeat = 1¼ in. (3 cm) wide x 4¼ in. (11 cm) high

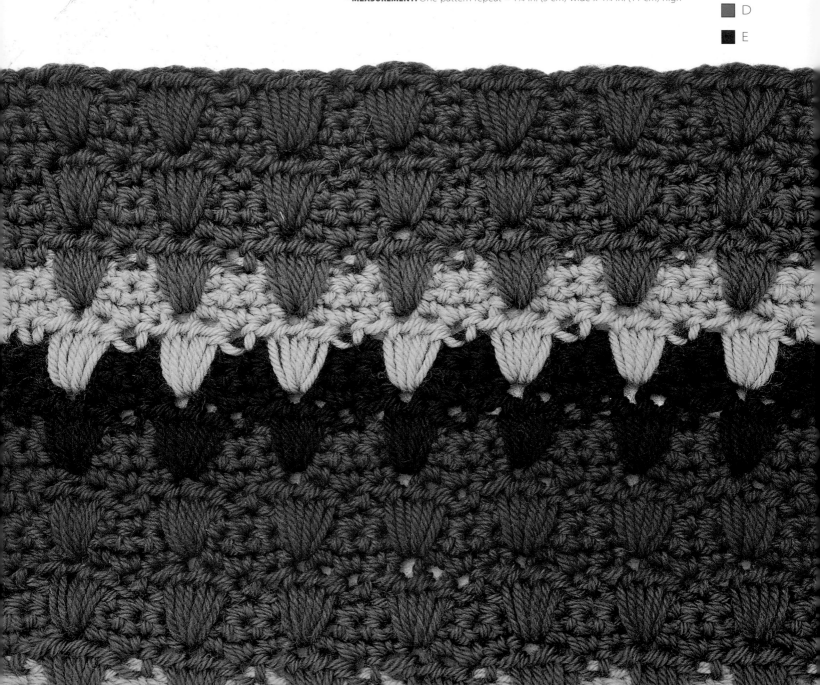

Method

FOUNDATION CHAIN: With Color A, ch a multiple of 4 + 3, turn foundation ch.

ROW 1: Ch 1, sc in 2nd ch from hook, * sc in each of next 2 ch, ch 1, skip 1 ch, sc in next ch; rep from * until 2 ch remain, sc in each of last 2 ch, turn.

ROW 2: Ch 1, sc in same place, sc in next st, * sc in next st, ch 1, skip 1 st, sc in each of next 2 sts; rep from * until 1 st remains, sc in last st, turn.

ROW 3: Ch 1, sc in same place, * sc in each of next 2 sts, ch 1, skip 1 st, sc in next st; rep from * until 2 sts remain, sc in each of last 2 sts, end Color A, turn.

ROW 4: Join Color B, ch 1, sc in same place, sc in next st, * 3 dc into skipped ch of Row 1, skip 3 sts of current row, sc in next st; rep from * until 1 st remains, sc in last st, turn.

ROW 5: Ch 1, sc in same place, * sc in each of next 2 sts, ch 1, skip 1 st, sc in next st; rep from * until 2 sts remain, sc in each of last 2 sts, turn.

ROW 6: Rep Row 2.

ROW 7: Rep Row 3, end Color B.

ROW 8: Join Color C, ch 1, sc in same, sc in next st, * 3 dc into middle dc 4 rows below, skip 3 sts of current row, sc in next st; rep from * until 1 st remains, sc in last st, turn.

ROWS 9–11: Rep Rows 5–7, end Color C.

ROWS 12–15: Rep Rows 8–11 using Color D.

ROWS 16–19: Rep Rows 8–11 using Color E. Rep Rows 8–11, changing colors every 4 rows as established.

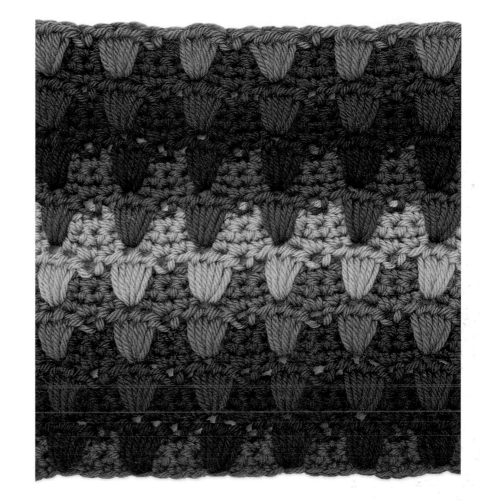

Indigo Vs

Follow instructions using alternative colors.

- A
- B
- C
- D
- E

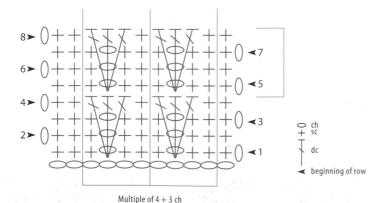

ch
sc

dc

◄ beginning of row

Multiple of 4 + 3 ch

Compact Chevrons

- **SKILL LEVEL:** Beginner
- **MEASUREMENT:** One pattern repeat =
  1¼ in. (3 cm) wide x 2 in. (5 cm) high

SPECIAL STITCH:

sc2tog: On Row 1 only, leaving sts unfinished, sc in next ch, skip 1 ch, sc in next ch, yo and draw through all loops on hook.
On all other rows, leaving sts unfinished, sc in next st, skip 1 st, sc in next st, yo and draw through all loops on hook.

■ A
■ B
■ C
☐ D
■ E

Method

FOUNDATION CHAIN: With Color A, ch a multiple of 6 + 1, turn foundation ch.

ROW 1: Ch 1, 2 sc in 2nd ch from hook, * sc in next st, sc2tog, sc in next st **, 3 sc in next st; rep from * until 6 ch remain, rep from * to ** once, 2 sc in last st, end Color A, turn.

ROW 2: Join Color B, ch 1, 2 sc in same place, sc in next st, sc2tog, sc in next st, * 3 sc in next st, sc in next st, sc2tog, sc in next st; rep from * until 1 st remains, 2 sc in last st, end Color B, turn.

ROW 3: Join Color C, ch 1, 2 sc in same place, * sc in next st, sc2tog, sc in next st **, 3 sc in next st; rep from * until 6 sts remain, rep from * to ** once, 2 sc in last st, end Color C, turn.

ROW 4: Rep Row 2 using Color D.

ROW 5: Rep Row 3 using Color E.

Rep Rows 2–3 for pattern, changing color each row.

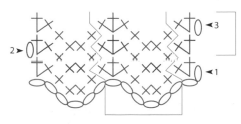

Multiple of 6 + 1 ch

⟨2 beginning of row⟩
⟨1⟩
⟨3⟩

○ ch
+ sc
×× sc2tog
◄ beginning of row

Contrast Ripple

Follow instructions using alternative colors:

ROWS 1–4: Color A
ROWS 5–6: Color B
ROW 7: Color C
ROW 8: Color B
ROW 9: Color A
ROWS 10–13: Color C
ROWS 14–17: Color D
ROW 18: Color A
ROW 19: Color D
ROW 20: Color C
ROW 21: Color A
Rep Rows 2–21 for pattern.

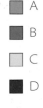

■ A
■ B
□ C
■ D

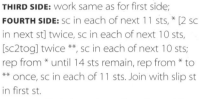

PROJECT
Afghan: Ice-cream Sundae

- **SKILL LEVEL:** Beginner
- **MEASUREMENT:** One pattern repeat =
  9 in. (23 cm) wide x 9 in. (23 cm) high
  Finished size = 12 ft 2 in. (3.7 m) x 5 ft 5 in.
  (1.65 m)
- **HOOK SIZE:** J-10 (6 mm)
- **YARN WEIGHT:** Worsted
- **YARN AMOUNT:** A: 290 yd (265 m); B: 204 yd
  (187 m); C: 207 yd (189 m); D: 190 yd (174 m);
  E: 212 yd (194 m); F: 204 yd (187 m); G: 211 yd
  (193 m); H: 196 yd (179 m); I 201 yd (184 m)

SPECIAL STITCH:

hdc2tog: Leaving sts unfinished, hdc in next
2 sts, yo and draw through all loops on hook.
dc2tog: On Row 1, leaving sts unfinished, dc
in next 2 ch, yo and draw through all loops
on hook. On all other rows, leaving sts
unfinished, dc in next 2 sts, yo and draw
through all loops on hook.
tr2tog: Leaving last two loops of sts
unfinished, tr in next 2 sts, yo and draw
through all loops on hook.

Method

FOUNDATION CHAIN: With Color A, ch 182.
ROW 1: Ch 3 (counts as 1 dc), dc in 4th ch
from hook, * dc in each of next 10 ch,
[dc2tog in each of next 2 ch] twice, dc in
each of next 10 ch **, [2 dc in next ch] twice;
rep from * until 25 ch remain, rep from * to **
once, 2 dc in last ch, end Color A, turn.
ROW 2: Join Color B, ch 2 (counts as 1 hdc),

hdc in same place, hdc in each of next 10 sts,
[hdc2tog] twice, hdc in each of next 10 sts, *
[2 hdc in next st] twice, hdc in each of next
10 sts, [hdc2tog] twice, hdc in each of next
10 sts; rep from * until 1 st remains, 2 hdc in
last st, end Color B, turn.
ROW 3: Join Color C, ch 4 (counts as 1 tr), tr
in same place, * tr in each of next 10 sts,
[tr2tog] twice, tr in each of next 10 sts **,
[2 tr in next st] twice; rep from * until 25 sts
remain, rep from * to ** once, 2 tr in last st,
end Color D, turn.
ROW 4: Join Color D and rep Row 2.
ROW 5: Join Color E, ch 3 (counts as 1 dc),
dc in same place, * dc in each of next 10 sts,
[dc2tog] twice, dc in each of next 10 sts,
[2 dc in next st] twice; rep from * until 25 sts
remain, rep from * to ** once, 2 dc in last st,
end Color E, turn.
Rep Rows 2–5 for pattern, changing color
each row until 63 rows have been worked,
ending with Color I.

EDGING:

With Color A, join yarn in first ch of
Foundation Chain, ch 1 and 3 sc in
same place;
FIRST SIDE: 2 sc around each dc, 1 sc around
each hdc, 3 sc around each tr to the next
corner, 3 sc in corner;
SECOND SIDE: * sc in each of next 10 sts,
[sc2tog] twice, sc in each of next 10 sts **,
[2 sc in next st] twice; rep from * 5 times,
rep from * to ** once, 3 sc in corner;

THIRD SIDE: work same as for first side;
FOURTH SIDE: sc in each of next 11 sts, * [2 sc
in next st] twice, sc in each of next 10 sts,
[sc2tog] twice **, sc in each of next 10 sts;
rep from * until 14 sts remain, rep from * to
** once, sc in each of 11 sts. Join with slip st
in first st.
ROUND 2: Ch 1, * 1 sc in each st along side,
3 sc in corner st; rep from * twice, 2 sc in
next st, sc in each st to last st, 2 sc in last st.
Join with slip st in first st.

Coral Reef

Follow instructions for blanket, repeating
Rows 2–5 and changing color each row.

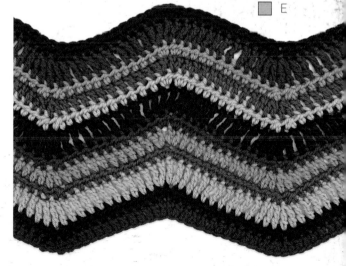

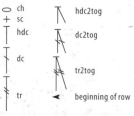

Multiple of 26 ch

Hot Star

- **SKILL LEVEL:** Beginner
- **MEASUREMENT:** One pattern repeat =
  8¾ in. (22 cm) wide x 8¾ in. (22 cm) high

SPECIAL STITCH:

dc2tog: On Round 3 only, leaving sts unfinished, dc in next 2 sts, yo and draw through all loops on hook. On all other rows, leaving sts unfinished, dc in next st, skip 1 st, dc in next st, yo and draw through all loops on hook.

A
B
C
D

Method

FOUNDATION CHAIN: With Color A, ch 6 and join with sl st in first ch to form a ring.

ROUND 1: Ch 3 (counts as 1 dc), 2 dc in ring, [ch 2, 3 dc in ring] 4 times, ch 2, join with sl st in top of first st—15 dc and 5 ch-sp.

ROUND 2: Sl st in next dc, [skip 1 st, (2 dc, tr, ch 2, tr, 2 dc) in ch-2 sp, skip 1 st, sl st in next st] 5 times, end Color A—30 dc and 5 ch-sp.

ROUND 3: Join Color B in ch-2 sp, ch 3 (counts as 1 dc), (dc, ch 2, 2 dc) in same place, * dc in each of next 2 sts, dc2tog, dc in each of next 2 sts **, (2 dc, ch 2, 2 dc) in ch-2 sp; rep from * 3 times, rep from * to ** once, join with sl st in first st—45 dc and 5 ch-sp.

ROUND 4: Ch 3 (counts as 1 dc), dc in next st, * (3 dc, ch 2, 3 dc) in ch-2 sp, dc in each of next 3 sts, dc2tog **, dc in each of next 3 sts; rep from * 3 times, rep from * to ** once, dc in next st, join with sl st in top of first st, end Color B—65 dc and 5 ch-sp.

ROUND 5: Join Color C in ch-2 sp, ch 3 (counts as 1 dc), (dc, ch 2, 2 dc) in same ch-2 sp, * dc in each of next 5 sts, dc2tog, dc in each of next 5 sts **, (2 dc, ch 2, 2 dc) in ch-2 sp; rep from * 3 times, rep from * to ** once, join with sl st in top of first st, end Color C—75 dc and 5 ch-sp.

ROUND 6: Join Color D in ch-2 sp, ch 3 (counts as 1 dc), (2 dc, ch 2, 3 dc) in same ch-2 sp, * dc in each of next 6 sts, dc2tog, dc in each of next 6 sts **, (3 dc, ch 2, 3 dc) in ch-2 sp; rep from * 3 times, rep from * to ** once, join with sl st in first st, end Color D—95 dc and 5 ch-sp.

ROUND 7: Rep Round 5 using Color A, working 1 more dc between ch-2 sp and dc2tog in each rep.

ROUND 8: Rep Round 4 using Color A, working 1 more dc between ch-2 sp and dc2tog in each rep.

Rep Rounds 5–8 for pattern, working 1 more dc between ch-2 sp and dc2tog in each rep.

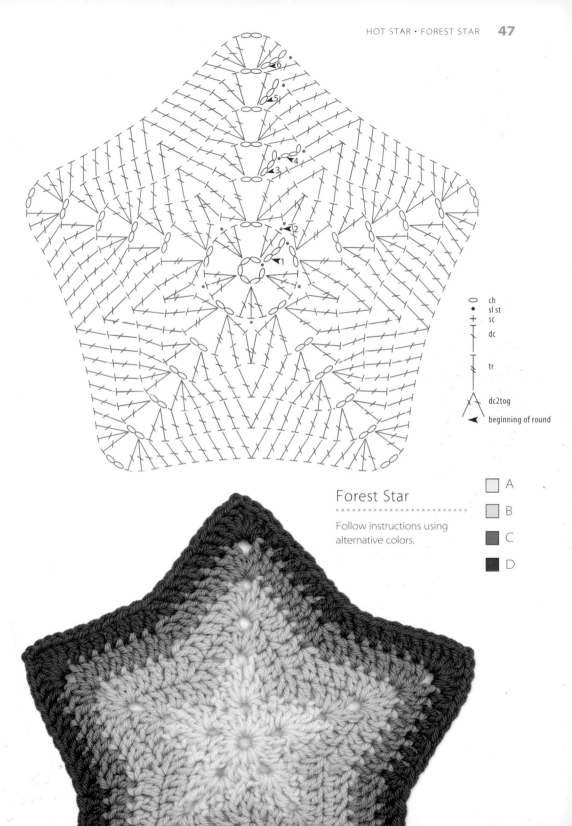

	ch
•	sl st
+	sc
	dc
	tr
	dc2tog
◄	beginning of round

Forest Star

Follow instructions using alternative colors.

☐	A
☐	B
■	C
■	D

Arcade

A

B

C

D

- **SKILL LEVEL:** Beginner
- **MEASUREMENT:** One pattern repeat =
  8¾ in. (22 cm) wide x 8¾ in. (22 cm) high

SPECIAL STITCH:

sc2tog: Leaving sts unfinished, sc in next 2 sts, yo and draw through all loops on hook.

sc2tog over 3 sts: Leaving sts unfinished, sc in next st, skip 1 st, sc in next st, yo and draw through all loops on hook.

Method

FOUNDATION RING: With Color A, ch 6 and join with sl st in first ch to form a ring.

ROUND 1: Ch 3 (counts as 1 dc), dc in ring, [ch 1, 2 dc in ring, ch 2, 2 dc in ring] 3 times, ch 1, 2 dc in ring, ch 2, join with sl st in top of first st, end Color A.

ROUND 2: Join Color B in ch-1 sp, ch 3 (counts as 1 dc), 2 dc in same place, * sc2tog, 6 dc in ch-2 sp, sc2tog **, 3 dc in ch-1 sp; rep from * twice more, then from * to ** once, join with sl st in top of first st, end Color B.

ROUND 3: Join Color C in center st of beginning 3-dc group, ch 3 (counts as 1 dc), 2 dc in same place, * sc2tog over 3 sts, dc in next st, [3 dc in next st] twice, dc in next st, sc2tog over 3 sts **, 3 dc in next st; repeat from * twice more, then from * to ** once, join with sl st in top of first st, end Color C.

ROUND 4: Join Color D in center st of beginning 3-dc group, ch 3 (counts as 1 dc), 4 dc in same place, * sc2tog over 3 sts, dc in each of next 2 sts, [3 dc in next st] twice, dc in each of next 2 sts, sc2tog over 3 sts **, 5 dc in next st; rep from * twice more, then from * to ** once, join with sl st in top of first st, end Color D.

ROUND 5: Join Color B in center st of beginning 5-dc group, ch 3 (counts as 1 dc), 2 dc in same place, * dc in next st, sc2tog over 3 sts, dc in each st to 3rd st of corner 3-dc group, [3 dc in next st] twice, dc in each st to 1 st before decrease, sc2tog over 3 sts, dc in next st **, 3 dc in next st; rep from * twice more, then from * to ** once, join with sl st in top of first st, end Color B.

ROUND 6: Join Color C in center st of beginning 3-dc group, ch 3 (counts as 1 dc), 2 dc in same place, * dc in next st, sc2tog over 3 sts, dc in each st to 3rd st of corner 3-dc group, [3 dc in next st] twice, dc in each st to 1 st before decrease, sc2tog over 3 sts, dc in next st **, 3 dc in next st; rep from * twice more, then from * to ** once, join with sl st in top of first st, end Color C.

ROUND 7: Join Color A in center st of beginning 3-dc group, ch 3 (counts as 1 dc), 4 dc in same place, * dc in next st, sc2tog over 3 sts, dc in each st to 3rd st of corner 3-dc group, [3 dc in next st] twice, dc in each st to 1 st before decrease, sc2tog over 3 sts, dc in next st **, 5 dc in next st; rep from * twice more, then from * to ** once, join with sl st in top of first st, end Color A.

Repeat Rounds 5–7, alternating Color A and Color D on repeats of Round 7.

Marrakesh

Follow instructions using alternative colors:

ROUND 1: Color A	**ROUND 5:** Color B
ROUND 2: Color B	**ROUND 6:** Color C
ROUND 3: Color C	**ROUND 7:** Color A
ROUND 4: Color A	Repeat Rounds 5–7 for pattern.

☐ A
◻ B
■ C

○	ch
•	sl st
+	sc
┼	dc
⋈	sc2tog
◄	beginning of round

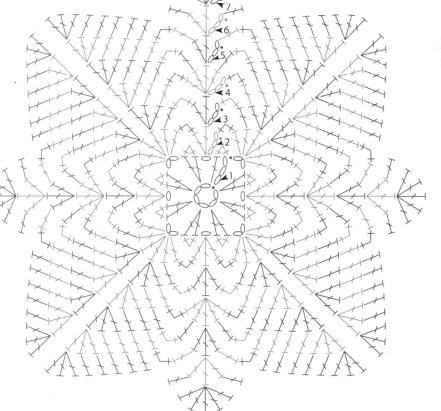

Bright Burst

- **SKILL LEVEL:** Beginner
- **MEASUREMENT:** One pattern repeat =
  9½ in. (24 cm) wide x 9½ in. (24 cm) high

SPECIAL STITCH:
sc3tog: Leaving sts unfinished, sc in next 3 sts, yo and draw through all loops on hook.
dc3tog: Leaving sts unfinished, dc in next 3 sts, yo and draw through all loops on hook.

☐ A
■ B
■ C
■ D

Method

FOUNDATION RING: With Color A, make a Magic Ring.

ROUND 1: Ch 3 (counts as 1 dc), 11 dc in ring, join with sl st in top of first st, end Color A.

ROUND 2: Join Color B, ch 3 (counts as 1 dc), dc in same place, 2 dc in each st around, join with sl st in top of first st, end Color B.

ROUND 3: Join Color C, ch 3 (counts as 1 dc), dc in same place, [dc in next st, 2 dc in next st] 11 times, dc in next st, join with sl st in top of first st, end Color C.

ROUND 4: Join Color D, ch 1 and sc in same place, [skip 2 sts, (3 dc, ch 2, 3 dc) in next st, skip 2 sts, sc in next st] 5 times, skip 2 sts, (3 dc, ch 2, 3 dc) in next st, skip 2 sts, join with sl st in top of first st.

ROUND 5: Ch 1 and sc in same place, [sc in each st to ch-sp, (sc, ch 2, sc) in ch-sp] 6 times, sc in each of next 3 sts, join with sl st in top of first st, end Color D.

ROUND 6: Join Color A in ch-2 sp, ch 3 (counts as 1 dc), (dc, ch 2, 2 dc) in same place, [dc tbl in each of next 3 sts, dc3tog tbl, dc tbl in each of next 3 sts, (2 dc, ch 2, 2 dc) in ch-sp] 5 times, dc tbl in each of next 3 sts, dc3tog tbl, dc tbl in each of next 3 sts, join with sl st in top of first st, end Color A.

ROUND 7: Join Color B in ch-2 sp, ch 1, [(sc, ch 2, sc) in ch-2 sp, sc in each st to 1 st before decrease, sc3tog, sc in each st to ch-sp] 6 times, join with sl st in top of first st, end Color B.

ROUND 8: Join Color C in ch-2 sp, ch 3 (counts as 1 dc), (dc, ch 2, 2 dc) in ch-2 sp, [dc in each st to 1 st before decrease, dc3tog, dc in each st to ch-sp, (2 dc, ch 2, 2 dc) in ch-2 sp] 5 times, dc in each st to 1 st before decrease, dc3tog, dc in each st to end of round, join with sl st in top of first st, end Color C.

Repeat Rounds 7 and 8 for pattern, changing colors each round.

Floral Pop

Follow instructions using alternative colors.

A

B

C

D

○	ch
•	sl st
+	sc
	dc
	dc tbl
	dc3tog tbl

sc3tog
dc3tog
◄ beginning of round

Jasmine

- **SKILL LEVEL:** Beginner
- **MEASUREMENT:** One pattern repeat = 9¾ in. (25 cm) wide x 9¾ in. (25 cm) high

SPECIAL STITCH:

sc2tog: Leaving sts unfinished, sc in next ch-sp, skip 1 st, sc in next ch-sp, yo and draw through all loops on hook.

A
B
C

Method

FOUNDATION RING: With Color A, make a Magic Ring.

ROUND 1: Ch 4 (counts as 1 dc, ch 1), [dc into ring, ch 1] 9 times, join with sl st in 3rd of beginning-ch, end Color A.

ROUND 2: Join Color B in ch-1 sp, ch 3 (counts as 1 dc), 2 dc in same place, ch 1, [3 dc in next ch sp, ch 1] 9 times, join with sl st in top of beginning-ch, end Color B.

ROUND 3: Join Color C in ch-1 sp, ch 1 and sc in same place, * skip 3 sts, (3 tr, ch 2, 3 tr) in next ch-sp, skip 3 sts **, sc in next ch-sp; rep from * 3 times, rep from * to ** once, join with sl st in beginning-ch, end Color C.

ROUND 4: Join Color A in ch-2 sp, ch 3 (counts as 1 dc), (2 dc, ch 3, 3 dc) in same place, * ch 1, skip 1 st, 3 dc in next st, ch 1, skip 1 st, sc in next st, ch 1, skip 1 st, 3 dc in next st, ch 1, skip 1 st **, (3 dc, ch 3, 3 dc) in ch-sp; rep from * 3 times, rep from * to ** once, join with sl st in top of beginning-ch, end Color A.

ROUND 5: Join Color B in next ch-3 sp, ch 3 (counts as 1 dc), (2 dc, ch 3, 3 dc) in same place, * ch 1, skip 1 st, 3 dc in next st, ch 1, skip 1 st, [3 dc in ch-1 sp, ch 1] to last ch-1 before an sc in last round, sc2tog, [ch 1, 3 dc in ch-1 sp] until no ch-1 sp remain before next ch 3 sp, ch 1, skip 1 st, 3 dc in next st, ch 1, skip 1 st **, (3 dc, ch 3, 3 dc) in ch-3 sp; rep from * 3 times, rep from * to ** once, join with sl st in top of beginning-ch, end Color B. Repeat Round 5, changing color each round.

Periwinkle

Follow instructions using alternative colors.

Key:
- ⬭ ch
- • sl st
- + sc
- ∫ dc
- ∫ tr
- ⋀ sc2tog
- ◄ beginning of round

- ☐ A
- ☐ B
- ☐ C

Fall Leaves

- **SKILL LEVEL:** Beginner
- **MEASUREMENT:** One pattern repeat =
  4¼ in. (11 cm) wide x 5½ in. (14 cm) high

SPECIAL STITCH:

dc2tog: Leaving sts unfinished, dc in next 2 ch or sts, yo and draw through all loops on hook.

A
B
C
D

Method

FOUNDATION CHAIN: With Color A, ch a multiple of 28, turn foundation chain.

ROW 1: Ch 3 (counts as 1 dc), 2 dc in 4th ch from hook, * [ch 2, skip 2 ch, dc in each of next 2 ch] twice, ch 2, skip 2 ch, dc2tog, skip 2 ch, dc2tog, [ch 2, skip 2 ch, dc in each of next 2 ch] twice, ch 2, skip 2 ch **, 2 dc in next ch, ch 2, 2 dc in next ch; rep from * to last 27 ch, rep from * to ** once, 3 dc in last ch, end Color A, do not turn.

ROW 2: Join Color B in first st of last row, ch 3 (counts as 1 dc), 2 dc in same place, * [ch 2, skip 2 sts, dc into each of 2 skipped ch 2 rows below] twice, ch 2, skip 2 sts, dc2tog into skipped ch 2 rows below, skip 2 sts, dc2tog into skipped ch 2 rows below, [ch 2, skip 2 sts, dc into each of 2 skipped ch 2 rows below] twice, ch 2, skip 2 sts **, (2 dc, ch 2, 2 dc) in ch-sp; rep from * to last 15 sts (not including ch-sp), rep from * to ** once, 3 dc in last st, end Color B, do not turn.

ROW 3: Join Color C in first st of last row, ch 3 (counts as 1 dc), 2 dc in same place, * [ch 2, skip 2 sts, dc into each of 2 skipped sts 2 rows below] twice, ch 2, skip 2 sts, dc2tog into each of 2 skipped sts 2 rows below, skip 2 sts, dc2tog into each of 2 skipped sts 2 rows below, [ch 2, skip 2 sts, dc into each of 2 skipped sts 2 rows below] twice, ch 2, skip 2 sts **, (2 dc, ch 2, 2 dc) in ch-sp; rep from * to last 15 sts (not including ch-sp), rep from * to ** once, 3 dc in last st, end Color C.

ROW 4: Repeat Row 3 using Color D.

ROW 5: Repeat Row 3 using Color A. Repeat Rows 2–5 for pattern.

ch

dc

dc2tog

beginning of row

Moss Bank

Follow instructions using alternative colors.

☐ A
☐ B
■ C
■ D

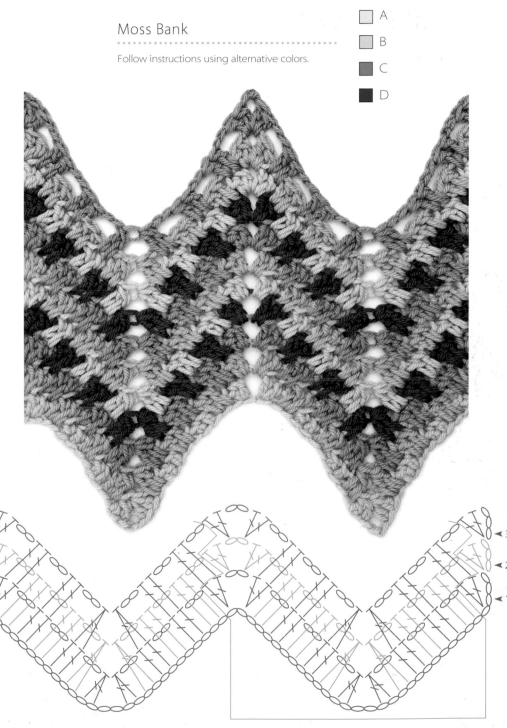

Multiple of 28 ch

Honeydew

- **SKILL LEVEL:** Beginner
- **MEASUREMENT:** One pattern repeat =
  6¼ in. (16 cm) wide x 5 in. (13 cm) high

SPECIAL STITCH:
dc2tog: Leaving sts unfinished, dc in next 2 sts, yo and draw through all loops on hook.

■ A
■ B
□ C

Method

FOUNDATION CHAIN: With Color A, ch a multiple of 29 + 14, turn foundation chain.

ROW 1: Ch 3 (counts as 1 dc), 2 dc in same place, * dc in each of next 2 ch, [dc2tog] 4 times, dc in each of next 2 ch **, 5 dc in next ch, dc in each of next 2 ch, hdc in each of next 2 ch, sc in each of next 2 ch, skip 3 ch, sc in each of next 2 ch, hdc in each of next 2 ch, dc in each of next 2 ch, 5 dc in next ch; rep from * to last 13 ch, rep from * to ** once, 3 dc in last ch, turn.

ROW 2: Ch 3 (counts as 1 dc), 2 dc tfl in same place, dc tfl in each of next 2 sts, [dc2tog tfl] 4 times, dc tfl in each of next 2 sts, * 5 dc tfl in next st, dc tfl in each of next 2 sts, hdc tfl in each of next 2 sts, sc tfl in each of next 2 sts, skip 4 sts, sc tbl in each of next 2 sts, hdc tfl in each of next 2 sts, dc tfl in each of next 2 sts, 5 dc tfl in next st, dc tfl in each of next 2 sts, [dc2tog tfl] 4 times, dc tfl in each of next 2 sts; rep from * to last st, 3 dc in last st, end Color A, turn.

ROW 3: Join Color B, ch 3 (counts as 1 dc), 2 dc in same place, * dc in each of next 2 sts, [dc2tog] 4 times, dc in each of next 2 sts **, 5 dc in next st, dc in each of next 2 sts, hdc in each of next 2 sts, sc in each of next 2 sts, skip 4 sts, sc in each of next 2 sts, hdc in each of next 2 sts, dc in each of next 2 sts, 5 dc in next st; rep from * to last 13 sts, rep from * to ** once, 3 dc in last st, turn.

ROW 4: Repeat Row 2, end Color B, turn.

ROWS 5–6: Repeat Rows 3–4 using Color C.

ROWS 7–8: Repeat Rows 3–4 using Color A. Rows 3–8 form the color pattern.

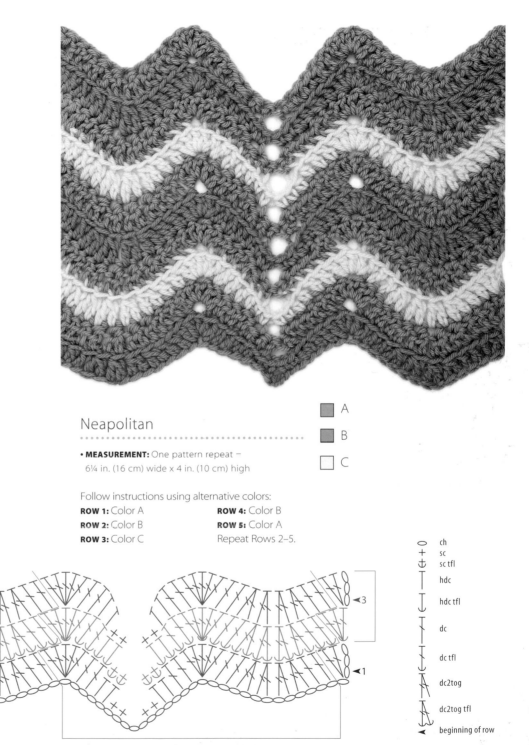

Neapolitan

	A
	B
	C

• **MEASUREMENT:** One pattern repeat – 6¼ in. (16 cm) wide x 4 in. (10 cm) high

Follow instructions using alternative colors:

ROW 1:	Color A	**ROW 4:**	Color B
ROW 2:	Color B	**ROW 5:**	Color A
ROW 3:	Color C		Repeat Rows 2–5.

○	ch
+	sc
⊎	sc tfl
T	hdc
	hdc tfl
	dc
	dc tfl
	dc2tog
	dc2tog tfl
◄	beginning of row

Multiple of 29 + 14 ch

Pink Denim

- **SKILL LEVEL:** Beginner
- **MEASUREMENT:** One pattern repeat = 2¾ in. (7 cm) wide x 2¼ in. (5.5 cm) high

SPECIAL STITCH:

sc2tog: Leaving sts unfinished, sc in next 2 sts, yo and draw through all loops on hook.

A
B
C
D

Method

FOUNDATION CHAIN: With Color A, ch a multiple of 16, turn foundation chain.

ROW 1: Ch 1 and 2 sc in same place, * sc in each of next 5 ch, [sc2tog] twice, sc in each of next 5 ch **, [2 sc in next ch] twice; rep from * to last 15 ch, rep from * to ** once, 2 sc in last ch, end Color A, do not turn.

ROW 2: Join Color B in first st of last row, ch 1 and 2 sc in same place, * [ch 1, skip 1 st, sc in next st] twice, ch 1, skip 1 st, [sc2tog] twice, [ch 1, skip 1 st, sc in next st] twice, ch 1, skip 1 st **, [2 sc in next st] twice; rep from * to last 15 sts, rep from * to ** once, 2 sc in last st, end Color B, do not turn.

ROW 3: Join Color C in first st of last row, ch 1 and 2 sc in same place, * [ch 1, skip 1 st, sc in ch-sp] twice, ch 1, skip 1 st, sc2tog into ch sp and next sc, sc2tog in next sc and ch-sp, [ch 1, skip 1 st, sc in ch-sp] twice, ch 1, skip 1 st **, [2 sc in next st] twice; rep from * to last 9 sts (not including ch sp), rep from * to ** once, 2 sc in last st, end Color C, do not turn.

ROW 4: Repeat Row 3 using Color D. Repeat Row 3, alternating colors every row.

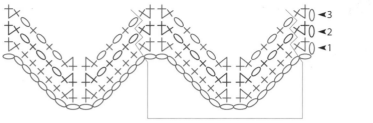

Multiple of 16 ch

○ ch
+ sc
⨉ sc2tog
◄ beginning of row

Vibrate

■ A
■ B
□ C
■ D

- **MEASUREMENT:** One pattern repeat = 6¼ in. (16 cm) wide x 4 in. (10 cm) high

Follow instructions using alternative colors:

ROW 1: Color A	**ROW 7:** Color C
ROW 2: Color B	**ROW 8:** Color B
ROW 3: Color C	**ROW 9:** Color A
ROW 4: Color A	**ROW 10:** Color D
ROW 5: Color D	**ROW 11:** Color A
ROW 6: Color A	Repeat Rows 2–11 for pattern.

Rhythm

- **SKILL LEVEL:** Beginner
- **MEASUREMENT:** One pattern repeat = 6¾ in. (17 cm) wide x 6¼ in. (16 cm) high

SPECIAL STITCH:

sc2tog: Leaving sts unfinished, sc in next st, skip 1 st, sc in next st, yo and draw through all loops on hook.

A
B
C
D
E
F
G

Method

FOUNDATION CHAIN: With Color A, ch a multiple of 34 + 17, turn foundation chain.

ROW 1 (RS): Ch 1 and 2 sc in same place, * [sc in each of next 2 ch, sc2tog over next 3 ch, sc in each of next 2 ch, 3 sc in next ch] twice, sc in each of next 7 ch, sc2tog over next 3 ch, sc in each of next 7 ch, 3 sc in next ch; rep from * to last 16 ch, sc in each of next 2 ch, sc2tog over next 3 ch, sc in each of next 2 ch, 3 sc in next ch, sc in each of next 2 ch, sc2tog over next 3 ch, sc in each of next 2 ch, 2 sc in last ch, turn.

ROW 2 (WS): Ch 1 and 2 sc in same place, sc in each of next 2 sts, sc2tog, sc in each of next 2 sts, 3 sc in next st, sc in each of next 2 sts, sc2tog, sc in each of next 2 sts, * 3 sc in next st, sc in each of next 7 sts, sc2tog, sc in each of next 7 sts, [3 sc in next st, sc in each of next 2 sts, sc2tog, sc in each of next 2 sts] twice; rep from * to last st, 2 sc in last st, end Color A, turn.

ROW 3 (RS): Join Color B, ch 1 and 2 sc in same place, * [sc in each of next 2 sts, sc2tog, sc in each of next 2 sts, 3 sc in next st] twice, sc in each of next 7 sts, sc2tog, sc in each of next 7 sts, 3 sc in next st; rep from * to last 16 sts, sc in each of next 2 sts, sc2tog, sc in each of next 2 sts, 3 sc in next st, sc in each of next 2 sts, sc2tog, sc in each of next 2 sts, 2 sc in last st, turn.

Repeat Rows 2–3 working two rows in each color.

For colors used on the cover, see page 128.

70s Groove

• **MEASUREMENT:** One pattern repeat = 6¼ in. (16 cm) wide x 4 in. (10 cm) high

Follow instructions using alternative colors.

A
B
C
D
E

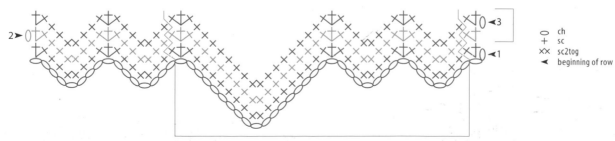

○ ch
+ sc
✕✕ sc2tog
◄ beginning of row

Multiple of 34 + 17 ch

Syrah

- **SKILL LEVEL:** Beginner
- **MEASUREMENT:** One pattern repeat = 6¼ in. (16 cm) wide x 4¼ in. (11 cm) high

SPECIAL STITCH:

sc2tog: Leaving sts unfinished, sc in next 2 sts, yo and draw through all loops on hook.

hdc2tog: Leaving sts unfinished, hdc in next 2 sts, yo and draw through all loops on hook.

dc2tog: Leaving sts unfinished, dc in next 2 ch or sts, yo and draw through all loops on hook.

A
B
C
D
E
F

Method

FOUNDATION CHAIN: With Color A, ch a multiple of 24 + 18, turn foundation chain.

ROW 1: Ch 3 (counts as 1 dc), 1 dc in 4th ch from hook, * dc in each of next 6 ch, [dc2tog] twice, dc in each of next 6 ch **, 3 dc in next ch, dc in next ch, [dc2tog] twice, dc in next ch, 3 dc in next ch; rep from * to last 17 ch, rep from * to ** once, 2 dc in last ch, end Color A, turn.

ROW 2: Join Color B, ch 2 (counts as 1 hdc), hdc in same place, hdc in each of next 6 sts, [hdc2tog] twice, hdc in each of next 6 sts, * 3 hdc in next st, hdc in next st, [hdc2tog] twice, hdc in next st, 3 hdc in next st, hdc in each of next 6 sts, [hdc2tog] twice, hdc in each of next 6 sts; rep from * to last st, 2 hdc in last st, end Color B, turn.

ROW 3: Join Color C, ch 1 and 2 sc in same place, * sc in each of next 6 sts, [sc2tog] twice, sc in each of next 6 sts **, 3 sc in next st, sc in next st, [sc2tog] twice, sc in next st, 3 sc in next st; rep from * to last 17 sts, rep from * to ** once, 2 sc in last st, end Color C, turn.

ROW 4: Join Color D, ch 3 (counts as 1 dc), dc in same place, dc in each of next 6 sts, [dc2tog] twice, dc in each of next 6 sts, * 3 dc in next st, dc in next st, [dc2tog] twice, dc in next st, 3 dc in next st, dc in each of next 6 sts, [dc2tog] twice, dc in each of next 6 sts; rep from * to last st, 2 dc in last st, end Color D, turn.

ROW 5: Join Color E, ch 2 (counts as 1 hdc), hdc in same place, * hdc in each of next 6 sts, [hdc2tog] twice, hdc in each of next 6 sts **, 3 hdc in next st, hdc in next st, [hdc2tog] twice, hdc in next st, 3 hdc in next st; rep from * to ** to last 17 sts, rep from * to ** once, 2 hdc in last st, end Color E, turn.

ROW 6: Join Color F, ch 1 and 2 sc in same place, sc in each of next 6 sts, [sc2tog] twice, sc in each of next 6 sts, * 3 sc in next st, sc in next st, [sc2tog] twice, sc in next st, 3 sc in next st, sc in each of next 6 sts, [sc2tog] twice, sc in each of next 6 sts; rep from * to last st, 2 sc in last st, end Color F, turn.

ROW 7: Join Color A, ch 3 (counts as 1 dc), dc in same place, * dc in each of next 6 sts, [dc2tog] twice, dc in each of next 6 sts **, 3 dc in next st, dc in next st, [dc2tog] twice, dc in next st, 3 dc in next st; rep from * to last 17 sts, rep from * to ** once, 2 dc in last st, end Color A, turn.
Repeat Rows 2–7 for pattern.

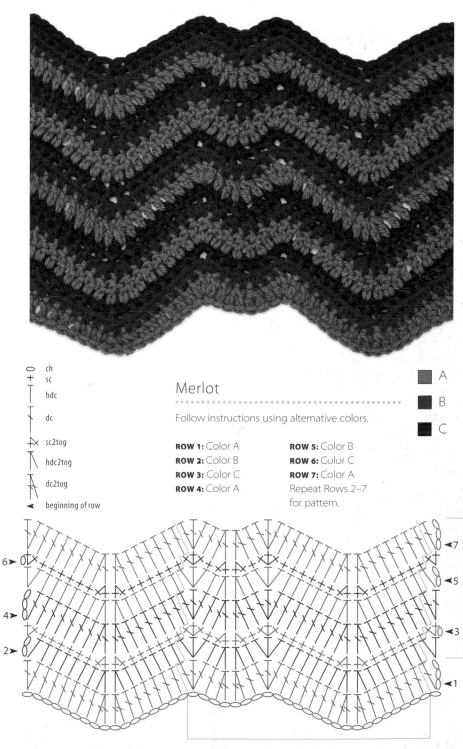

○	ch
+	sc
T	hdc
⊺	dc
⊁	sc2tog
⋏	hdc2tog
⋏	dc2tog
◄	beginning of row

■ A
■ B
■ C

Merlot

Follow instructions using alternative colors.

ROW 1: Color A

ROW 2: Color B

ROW 3: Color C

ROW 4: Color A

ROW 5: Color B

ROW 6: Color C

ROW 7: Color A
Repeat Rows 2–7
for pattern.

Multiple of 24 + 18 ch

PROJECT
Pillow: San Francisco

- **SKILL LEVEL:** Beginner
- **MEASUREMENT:** One pattern repeat = 2¾ in. (7 cm) wide x 4¼ in. (11 cm) high Finished size = see relevant cushion
- **HOOK SIZE:** H-8 (5 mm)
- **YARN WEIGHT:** Worsted
- **YARN AMOUNT:** 12 in. (30 cm) Pillow— A: 44 yd (45 m); B: 38 yd (35 m); C: 32 yd (29 m); D: 32 yd (29 m); E: 32 yd (29 m); F: 32 yd (29 m); G: 32 yd (29 m); H: 32 yd

(29 m); 18 in. (45 cm) Pillow—A: 85 yd (78 m); B: 77 yd (70 m); C: 67 yd (61 m); D: 67 yd (61 m); E: 67 yd (61 m); F: 67 yd (61 m); G: 67 yd (61 m); H: 67 yd (61 m); 20 in. (50 cm) Pillow—A: 123 yd (112 m); B: 112 yd (102 m); C: 100 yd (91 m); D: 100 yd (91 m); E: 100 yd (91 m); F: 100 yd (91 m); G: 100 yd (91 m)

- **ADDITIONAL MATERIALS:** 4 buttons for 12 in. (30 cm) cushion, 6 buttons for 18 in. (45 cm) cushion, 7 buttons for 20 in. (50 cm) cushion

SPECIAL STITCH:

dc2tog: On Row 1, leaving sts unfinished, dc in next ch, skip 2 ch, dc in next ch, yo and draw through all loops on hook.
dc3tog: Leaving sts unfinished, dc in next 3 sts, yo and draw through all loops on hook.

12 in. (30 cm) Pillow

FOUNDATION CHAIN: With Color A, ch 40, turn.

ROW 1: Ch 3 (counts as 1 dc), dc in 4th ch from hook, * dc in each of next 2 ch, dc2tog, dc in each of next 2 ch **, [2 dc in next ch] twice; rep from * until 9 ch remain, rep from * to ** once, 2 dc in last ch, end Color A, turn.

ROW 2: Join Color B, ch 3 (counts as 1 dc), dc in same place, dc in each of next 2 sts, dc3tog, dc in each of next 2 sts, * [2 dc in next st] twice, dc in each of next 2 sts, dc3tog, dc in each of next 2 sts; rep from * until 1 st remains, 2 dc in last st, end Color B, turn.

ROW 3: Join Color C, ch 3 (counts as 1 dc), dc in same place, * dc in each of next 2 sts, dc3tog, dc in each of next 2 sts **, [2 dc in next st] twice; rep from * until 8 sts remain, rep from * to ** once, 2 dc in last st, end Color C, turn.
Rep Rows 2–3, changing color each row until 42 rows have been worked, ending with Color B. Fasten off.

Fold piece like an envelope at Rows 8 and 28, overlapping the two ends so that Row 1 is above Row 41. Join Color A around st on Row 8 and Row 9, ch 1, working through both layers work 2 sc around each st to bottom edge. Fasten off. Rep along other side of cushion cover. Weave in ends.

Sew 4 buttons to top of Row 41, and use the ch-2 sp of the foundation row for buttonholes.

- ■ A
- ☐ B
- ■ C
- ■ D
- ☐ E
- ■ F
- ■ G
- ■ H

18 in. (45 cm) Pillow

With Color A, ch 60, work as for 12 in. (30 cm) cushion working in the above color sequence until a total of 58 rows have been worked, ending with Color B. Fasten off.

Fold piece like an envelope at Rows 13 and 40, overlapping the two ends so that Row 1 is above Row 57. Join Color A around st on Row 13 and Row 14, ch 1, working through both layers, work 2 sc around each st to bottom edge. Fasten off. Rep along other side of cushion cover. Weave in ends.

Sew 6 buttons to top of Row 56 and use the ch-2 sp of the foundation row for buttonholes.

- ■ A
- ■ B
- ☐ C
- ■ D
- ■ E
- ☐ F
- ☐ G
- ☐ H

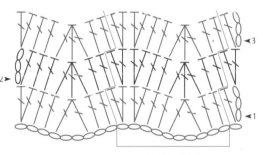

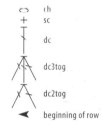

Multiple of 10 ch

20 in. (50 cm) Pillow

With Color A, ch 70, work as for 12 in. (30 cm) cushion working in the above color sequence until 65 rows have been worked, ending with Color B. Fasten off.

Fold piece like an envelope at Rows 14 and 44, overlapping the two ends so that Row 1 is above Row 64. Join Color A around st on Row 14 and Row 15, ch 1, working through both layers, work 2 sc around each st to bottom edge. Fasten off. Rep along other side of cushion cover. Weave in ends.

Sew 7 buttons to top of Row 64 and use the ch-2 sp of the foundation row for buttonholes.

- ☐ A
- ■ B
- ■ C
- ■ D
- ☐ E
- ☐ F
- ■ G

⌒ ch
+ sc
┼ dc
⋏ dc3tog
⋎ dc2tog
◄ beginning of row

Glade

Ch a multiple of 10 and work as for 12 in. (30 cm) cushion.

- ☐ A
- ■ B
- ■ C
- ■ D
- ■ E
- ■ F
- ☐ G

Berry Ripple

- **SKILL LEVEL:** Intermediate
- **MEASUREMENT:** One pattern repeat = 4¼ in. (11 cm) wide x 4¼ in. (11 cm) high

◼ A
◻ B
◼ C

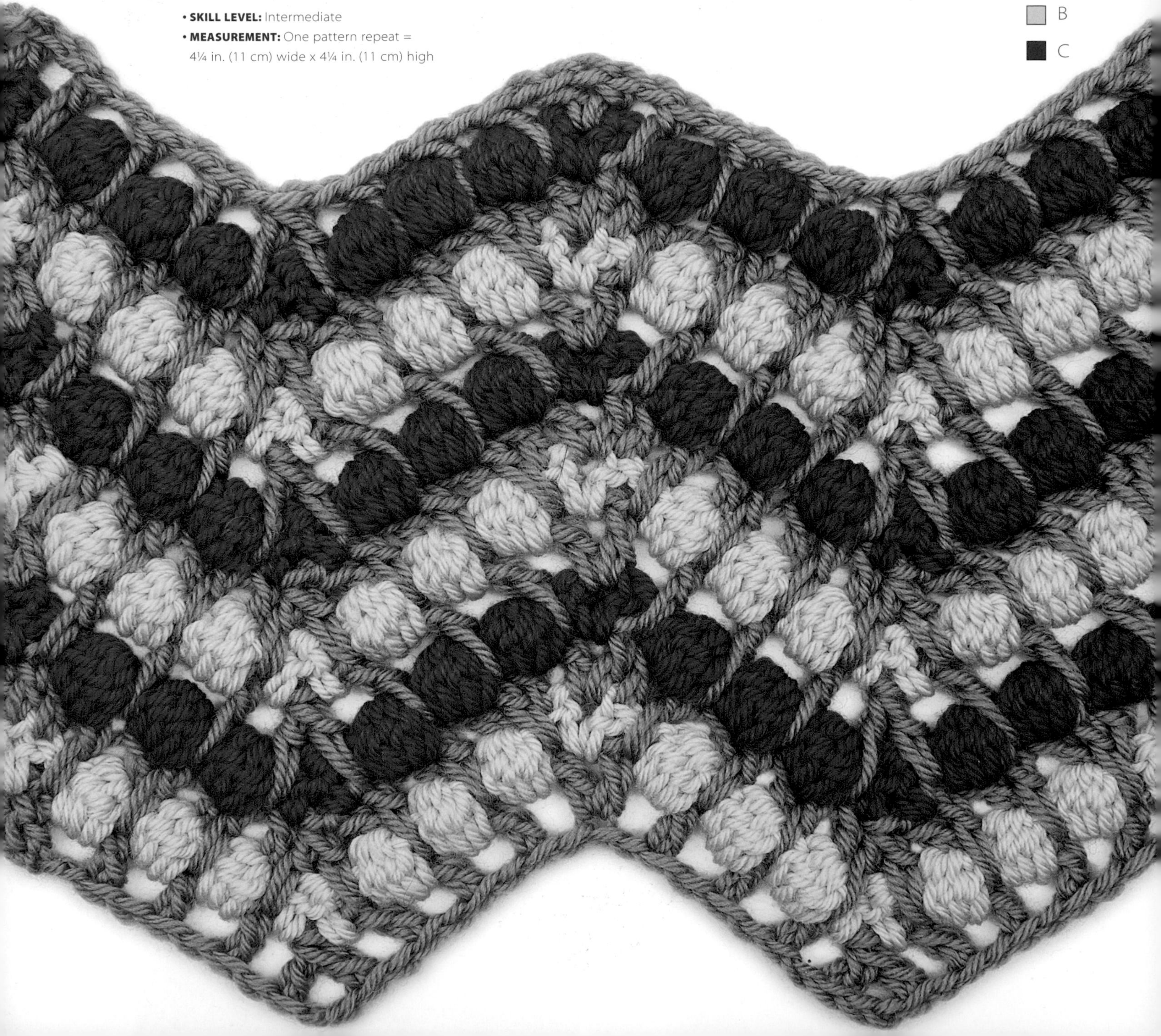

SPECIAL STITCH:

dc2tog On Row 1, leaving sts unfinished, dc in next ch, skip 2 ch, dc in next ch, yo and draw through all loops on hook. On all other rows, dc in next st, skip 1 st, dc in next st.

Berry Leaving sts unfinished, work 4 dc into ch-1 sp or st indicated, yo and draw through all loops on hook.

Method

FOUNDATION CHAIN: With Color A, ch a multiple of 19 + 1, turn foundation ch.

ROW 1: Ch 3 (counts as 1 dc), dc in 4th ch from hook, * [ch 1, skip 1 ch, dc in next ch] 3 times, ch 1, skip 1 ch, dc2tog, [ch 1, skip 1 ch, dc in next ch] 3 times, ch 1, skip 1 ch **, (dc, ch 1, dc) in next ch; rep from * until 19 ch remain, rep from * to ** once, 2 dc in last ch, end Color A, turn.

ROW 2: Join Color B, ch 3 (counts as 1 dc), dc in same place, [ch 1, skip 1 st, Berry in ch-1 sp] 3 times, ch 1, skip 1 st, dc2tog, [ch 1, skip 1 st, Berry in ch-1 sp] 3 times, ch 1, skip 1 st, * (dc, ch 1, dc) in ch-1 sp, [ch 1, skip 1 st, Berry in ch-1 sp] 3 times, ch 1, skip 1 st, dc2tog, [ch 1, skip 1 st, Berry in ch 1 sp] 3 times, ch 1; rep from * until 1 st remains, 2 dc in last st, end Color B, turn.

ROW 3: Join Color A, ch 3 (counts as 1 dc), dc in same place, * [dc in next st, dc over ch-1 sp into dc of Row 1] 3 times, dc in next st, dc2tog working into sts of Row 1, [dc in next st, dc over ch-1 sp into dc of Row 1] 3 times, dc in next st **, (dc, ch 1, dc) in ch-1 sp; rep from * until 10 sts remain, rep from * to ** once, 2 dc in last st, end Color A, turn.

ROW 4: Join Color C, ch 3 (counts as 1 dc), dc in same place, [ch 1, skip 1 st, Berry in next st] 3 times, ch 1, skip 1 st, dc2tog, [ch 1, skip 1 st, Berry in next st] 3 times, ch 1, skip 1 st, *(dc, ch 1, dc) in ch-1 sp, [ch 1, skip 1 st, Berry in next st] 3 times, ch 1, skip 1 st, dc2tog, [ch 1, skip 1 st, Berry in next st] 3 times, ch 1; rep from * until 1 st remains, 2 dc in last st, end Color C, turn.

ROW 5: Join Color A, ch 3 (counts as 1 dc), dc in same place, [ch 1, skip 1 st, dc over ch-1 sp into dc of Row 3] 3 times, ch 1, dc2tog working over ch-1 sp into dc of Row 3, [ch 1, skip 1 st, dc over ch-1 sp into dc of Row 3] 3 times, ch 1 **, (dc, ch 1, dc) in ch-1 sp; rep from * until 10 sts remain, rep from * to ** once, 2 dc in last st, end Color A, turn.

Rep Rows 2–5 for pattern.

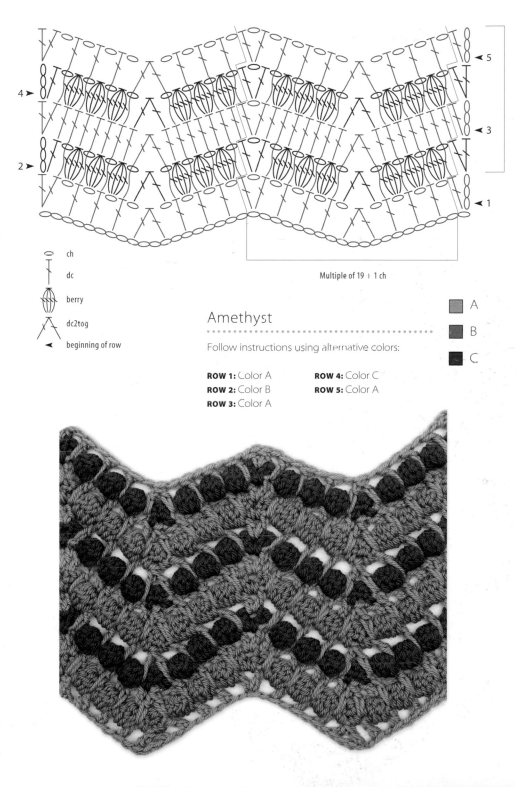

Multiple of 19 + 1 ch

⬯	ch
	dc
	berry
	dc2tog
◄	beginning of row

Amethyst

Follow instructions using alternative colors:

ROW 1: Color A   **ROW 4:** Color C
ROW 2: Color B   **ROW 5:** Color A
ROW 3: Color A

■ A
■ B
■ C

Lavender Layers

- **SKILL LEVEL:** Intermediate
- **MEASUREMENT:** One pattern repeat =
  3¼ in. (8 cm) wide x 7½ in. (19 cm) high

SPECIAL STITCH:

sc2tog: On Row 1 only, leaving sts unfinished, sc in next st, skip 2 ch, sc in next st, yo and draw through all loops on hook. On all other rows, leaving sts unfinished, sc in next st, skip 1 st, sc in next st, yo and draw through all loops on hook.
Bobble (B): Leaving sts unfinished, work 4 dc in same st, yo and draw through all loops on hook.

■ A
■ B
■ C
□ D
□ E
□ F

Method

FOUNDATION CHAIN: With Color A, ch a multiple of 17 + 1, turn foundation ch.

ROW 1 (WS): Ch 1, 2 sc in 2nd ch from hook, * sc in next 6 ch, sc2tog, sc in next 6 ch **, 3 sc in next ch; rep from * until 17 ch remain, rep from * to ** once, 2 sc in last ch, turn.

ROW 2 (RS): Ch 1 and 2 sc in same place, sc in next 6 sts, sc2tog, sc in next 6 sts, * 3 sc in next st, sc in next 6 sts, sc2tog, sc in next 6 sts; rep from * until 1 st remains, 2 sc in last st, turn.

ROW 3 (WS): Ch 1 and 2 sc in same place, * sc in next 6 sts, sc2tog, sc in next 6 sts **, 3 sc in next st; rep from * until 16 sts remain, rep from * to ** once, 2 sc in last st, turn.

ROW 4 (RS): Rep Row 2, end Color A.

ROW 5 (WS): Join Color B, ch 1 and 2 sc in same place, * sc in next 6 sts, sc2tog, sc in next 6 sts **, (sc, B, sc) in next st; rep from * until 16 sts remain, rep from * to ** once, 2 sc in last st, end Color B, turn.

ROW 6 (RS): Join Color A, ch 1 and 2 sc in same place, sc in next 6 sts, sc2tog, sc in next 6 sts, * 3 sc in top of Bobble, sc in next 6 sts, sc2tog, sc in next 6 sts; rep from * until 1 st remains, 2 sc in last st, end Color A, turn.

ROW 7 (WS): Join Color C, ch 1 and 2 sc in same place, * sc in next 6 sts, sc2tog, sc in next 6 sts **, 3 sc in next st, rep from *until 16 sts remain, rep from * to ** once, 2 sc in last st, turn.

ROWS 8–10 (RS): Rep Rows 2–4 using Color C.

ROW 11 (WS): Rep Row 5 using Color D.

ROW 12 (RS): Rep Row 6 using Color C.

ROWS 13–16 (WS): Rep Row 7 and Rows 2–4 using Color E.

ROW 17 (RS): Rep Row 5 using Color F.

ROW 18 (WS): Rep Row 6 using Color A.
Rep Rows 2–18 for pattern.

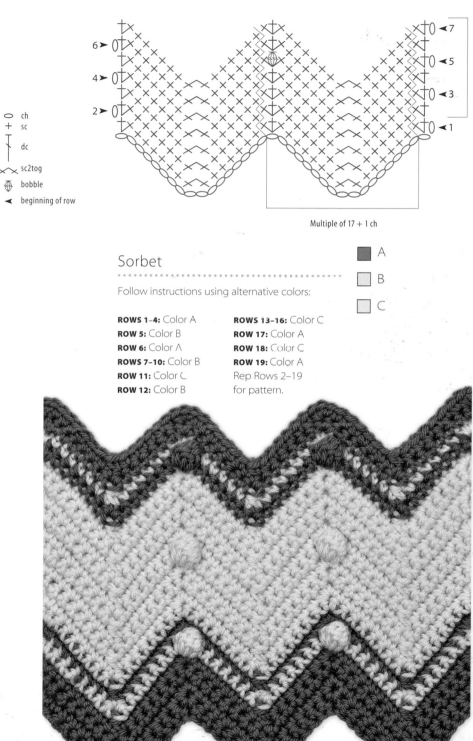

- ○ ch
- + sc
- ┿ dc
- ⤬ sc2tog
- ⬮ bobble
- ◄ beginning of row

Multiple of 17 + 1 ch

Sorbet

Follow instructions using alternative colors:

ROWS 1–4: Color A
ROW 5: Color B
ROW 6: Color A
ROWS 7–10: Color B
ROW 11: Color C
ROW 12: Color B

ROWS 13–16: Color C
ROW 17: Color A
ROW 18: Color C
ROW 19: Color A
Rep Rows 2–19 for pattern.

- ■ A
- □ B
- □ C

Pastel Posy

- **SKILL LEVEL:** Intermediate
- **MEASUREMENT:** One pattern repeat = 10¾ x 10¾ in. (27 x 27 cm)

SPECIAL STITCH:
dc2tog: Leaving sts unfinished, dc in next st, skip 1 st, dc in next st, yo and draw through all loops on hook.

☐ A
☐ B
☐ C
☐ D
■ E

Fuchsia Flower

Follow instructions using alternative colors.

☐ A
☐ B
■ C
■ D
■ E

Method

FOUNDATION CHAIN: With Color A, make a Magic Ring.

ROUND 1: Ch 3 (counts as 1 dc), 14 dc in ring, join with sl st in top of first st, end Color A—15 sts.

ROUND 2: Join Color B, ch 3 (counts as 1 dc), dc in same place, 2 dc in each dc around, join with sl st in top of first st, end Color B—30 sts.

ROUND 3: Join Color C, ch 3 (counts as 1 dc), dc in same place, [dc in next dc, 2 dc in next dc] 14 times, dc in last dc, join with sl st in top of first st, end Color C—45 sts.

ROUND 4: Join Color D, ch 1 and sc in same place, [sc in next dc, 2 sc in next dc, sc in next dc] 14 times, sc in next dc, 2 sc in last dc, join with sl st in top of first st, end Color D—60 sts.

ROUND 5: Join Color E, ch 1, sc in same place, * skip 2 sc, (2 dc, ch 1, 2 dc) in next sc, skip 2 sc, sc in next sc, skip 2 sc, (4 dc, ch 1, 4 dc) in next sc, skip 2 sc **, sc in next st; rep from * 3 times, rep from * to ** once, join with sl st in top of first st, end Color E—70 sts + 10 ch-1 sps.

ROUND 6: Join Color A in ch-1 sp of (2 dc, ch 1, 2 dc), ch 1 and sc in same place, * sc in each of next 2 sts, sc in dc of Round 3, sc in each of next 4 sts, sc in ch-1 sp, sc in each of next 4 sts **, sc in dc of Round 3, sc in each of next 2 sts, sc in ch-1 sp; rep from * 3 times, rep from * to ** once, join with sl st in top of first st, end Color A—80 sts.

ROUND 7: Join Color B, ch 3 (counts as 1 dc), 2 dc in same place, * dc in next sc, dc2tog, dc in each of next 3 sc, 3 dc in next sc, dc in each of next 3 sc, dc2tog, dc in next sc **, 3 dc in next sc; rep from * 3 times, rep from * to ** once, join with sl st in top of first st, end Color B.

ROUND 8: Join Color C in next dc, ch 3 (counts as 1 dc), 4 dc in same place, * dc in next dc, dc2tog, dc in each of next 3 sc, 5 dc in next dc, dc in each of next 3 sc, dc2tog, dc in next dc **, 5 dc in next dc; rep from * 3 times, rep from * to ** once, join with sl st in top of first st, end Color C—100 sts.

ROUND 9: Join Color A in 3rd of 5-dc group, ch 1, sc in same place, * sc in each of next 3 dc, sc into sc of Round 6, sc in each of next

11 dc, sc into sc of Round 6 **, sc in each of next 4 sts; rep from * 3 times, rep from * to ** once, sc in each of next 3 dc, join with sl st in top of first st, end Color A.

ROUND 10: Rep round 7 using Color D, working the extra stitches in double crochet.

ROUND 11: Rep round 8 using Color E—120 sts.

ROUND 12: Rep Round 9 using Color A. Rep Rounds 7–12 for pattern. You will be increasing four stitches on each repeat of Round 8. Work the new sts in dc on Rounds 7, 8, 10, and 11, and sc on Rounds 9 and 12, adding two sts between each increase and sc into the round three rounds below each time.

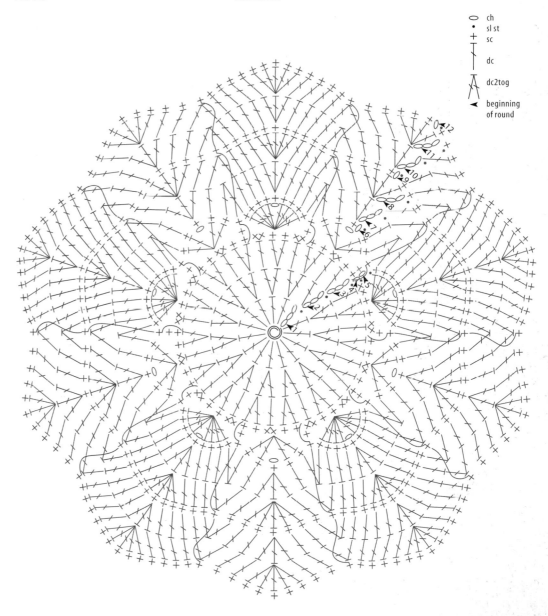

o	ch
•	sl st
+	sc
┬	dc
⋀	dc2tog
◄	beginning of round

Pumpkin Patch

- **SKILL LEVEL:** Intermediate
- **MEASUREMENT:** One pattern repeat = 3½ in. (9 cm) wide x 5 in. (13 cm) high

SPECIAL STITCH:

sc3tog: On Row 1 only, leaving sts unfinished, sc in next 3 ch, yo and draw through all loops on hook. On all other rows, leaving sts unfinished, sc in next 3 sts, yo and draw through all loops on hook.

Puff: Leaving sts unfinished, work 5 hdc in same st, yo and draw through all loops on hook.

- A
- B
- C
- D

Method

FOUNDATION CHAIN: With Color A, ch a multiple of 18 + 1, turn foundation ch.

ROW 1: Ch 1, 2 sc in 2nd ch from hook, * sc in next 7 ch, sc3tog, sc in next 7 ch **, 3 sc in next st; rep from * until 18 sts remain, rep from * to ** once, 2 sc in last st, turn.

ROW 2: Ch 1, 2 sc in same place, sc in next 7 sts, sc3tog, sc in next 7 sts, * 3 sc in next st, sc in next 7 sts, sc3tog, sc in next 7 sts; rep from * until 1 st remains, 2 sc in last st, end Color A, turn.

ROW 3: Join Color B, ch 1, 2 sc in same place, * sc in next 7 sts, sc3tog, sc in next 7 sts, ** 3 sc in next st; rep from * until 18 sts remain, rep from * to ** once, 2 sc in last st, turn.

ROW 4: Rep Row 2, end Color B.

ROW 5: Join Color C, ch 3 (counts as 1 dc), dc in same place, * [ch 1, skip 1 st, Puff in next st] 3 times, skip 2 sts, dc in next st, skip 2 sts, [Puff in next st, ch 1, skip 1 st] 3 times **, 3 dc in next st; rep from * until 18 sts remain, rep from * to ** once, 2 dc in last st, end Color C, turn.

ROW 6: Join Color D, ch 1, 2 sc in same place, [ch 1, Puff into skipped st of Row 4] 3 times, sc in dc, [Puff into skipped st of Row 4, ch 1] 3 times, * 3 sc in next st, [ch 1, Puff into skipped st of Row 4] 3 times, sc in dc, [Puff into skipped st of Row 4, ch 1] 3 times; rep from * until 1 st remains, 2 sc in last st, end Color D, turn.

ROW 7: Join Color A, ch 1, 2 sc in same place, * [sc in next st, sc in ch-1 sp] 3 times, sc in next st, sc3tog working into skipped st of Row 5, next st, and skipped st of Row 5, [sc in next st, sc in ch-1 sp] 3 times, sc in next st **, 3 sc in next st; rep from * until 10 sts remain, rep from * to ** once, 2 sc in last st, turn.

ROW 8: Rep Row 4, end Color A.

ROW 9: Join Color B and rep Row 3. Rep Rows 2–9 for pattern.

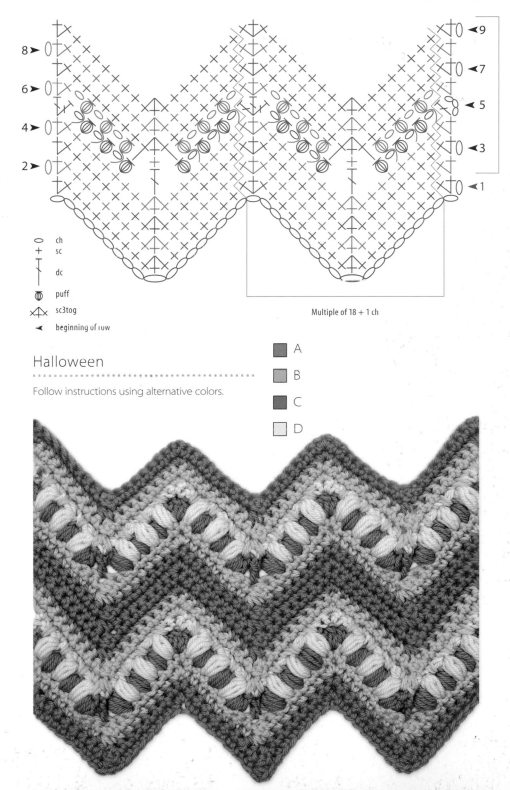

○ ch
+ sc
↑ dc
🟤 puff
△⋉✕ sc3tog
◄ beginning of row

Multiple of 18 + 1 ch

Halloween

Follow instructions using alternative colors.

■ A
■ B
■ C
□ D

4 ▶
2 ▶
◀ 5
◀ 3
◀ 1

ch
sl st
sc
dc
sc2tog
dc2tog
beginning of row

Multiple of 15 + 1 ch

Purple Picots

- **SKILL LEVEL:** Intermediate
- **MEASUREMENT:** One pattern repeat =
  3½ in. (9 cm) wide x 4 in. (10 cm) high

SPECIAL STITCH:

sc2tog: Leaving sts unfinished, sc in next
2 sts, yo and draw through all loops on hook.

dc2tog: On Row 1 only, leaving sts unfinished,
dc in next 2 ch, yo and draw through all
loops on hook. On all other rows, leaving
sts unfinished, dc in next 2 sts, yo and draw
through all loops on hook.

Picot Petals: Ch 6, sl st in last sc, ch 6, sl st in
last sc, ch 6, sl st in last sc.

Method

FOUNDATION CHAIN: With Color A, ch a
multiple of 15 + 1, turn foundation ch.

ROW 1: Ch 3 (counts as 1 dc), dc in 4th ch
from hook, * dc in next 5 ch, [dc2tog] twice,
dc in next 5 ch **, 3 dc in next ch; rep from *
until 15 ch remain, rep from * to ** once,
2 dc in last ch, turn.

ROW 2: Ch 1, 2 sc in same place, sc in
next 5 sts, [sc2tog] twice, sc in next 5 sts,
* 3 sc in next st, sc in next 5 sts, [sc2tog]
twice, sc in next 5 sts; rep from * until 1 st
remains, 2 sc in last st, end Color A, turn.

ROW 3: Join Color B, ch 1, 2 sc in same place,
* sc in next 5 sts, [sc2tog] twice, sc in next
5 sts **, (2 sc, Picot Petals, sc) in next st; rep
from * until 15 sts remain, rep from * to **
once, 2 sc in last st, end Color B, turn.

ROW 4: Join Color C, ch 1 and 2 sc in same
place, sc in next 5 sts, [sc2tog] twice, sc in
next 5 sts, * ch 2, skip sc with Picot Petals, sc
in next 5 sts, [sc2tog] twice, sc in next 5 sts;
rep from * until 1 st remains, 2 sc in last st,
end Color C, turn.

ROW 5: Join Color D, ch 3 (counts as 1 dc),
dc in same place, dc in next 5 sts **, [dc2tog]
twice, dc in next 4 sts, 5 dc in ch-2 sp, dc
in next 4 sts; rep from * until 10 sts remain,
[dc2tog] twice, dc in next 5 sts, 2 dc in last
st, turn.

ROW 6: Rep Row 3 using Color D. End Color D.

ROWS 7 & 8: Rep Rows 3–4.

ROW 9: Rep Row 5 using Color A.
Rep Rows 2–9 for pattern.

Shamrock Ripple

Follow instructions using alternative colors.

Red, Stripe, and Blue

- **SKILL LEVEL:** Intermediate
- **MEASUREMENT:** One pattern repeat =
  4¼ in. (11 cm) wide x 6¼ in. (16 cm) high

A
B
C
D
E

SPECIAL STITCH:

sc2tog: Leaving sts unfinished, sc in next 2 sts, yo and draw through all loops on hook.

dc2tog: On Row 1 only, leaving sts unfinished, dc in next 2 ch, yo and draw through all loops on hook. On all other rows, leaving sts unfinished, dc in next 2 sts, yo and draw through all loops on hook.

Bobble: Leaving sts unfinished, work 5 dc in next st, yo and draw through all loops on hook.

Method

FOUNDATION CHAIN: With Color A, ch a multiple
of 19 + 1, turn foundation ch.

ROW 1: Ch 3 (counts as 1 dc), dc in 4th ch from
hook, * dc in next 7 ch, [dc2tog] twice, dc in next
7 ch **, 3 dc in next ch; rep from * until 19 ch
remain, rep from * to ** once, 2 dc in last ch,
end Color A, turn.

ROW 2: Join Color B, ch 1, 2 sc in same place, sc in
next 7 sts, [sc2tog] twice, sc in next 7 sts, * 3 sc in
next st, sc in next 7 sts, [sc2tog] twice, sc in next
7 sts; rep from * until 1 st remains, 2 sc in last st,
end Color B, turn.

ROW 3 Join Color C, ch 1, 2 sc in same place, *
[Bobble in next st, sc in next st] 3 times, Bobble in
next st, [sc2tog] twice, [Bobble in next st, sc in
next st] 3 times, Bobble in next st **, 3 sc in next
st; rep from * until 19 sts remain, rep from * to **
once, 2 sc in last st, end Color C, turn.

ROW 4: Rep Row 2 using Color D.

ROW 5: Join Color E, ch 3 (counts as 1 dc), dc in
same place, * dc in next 7 sts, [dc2tog] twice, dc
in next 7 sts, ** 3 dc in next st; rep from * until
19 sts remain, rep from * to ** once, 2 dc in last st,
end Color F, turn

ROW 6: Rep Row 2 using Color D.

ROW 7: Join Color C, ch 1, 2 sc in same place,
* sc in next 7 sts, [sc2tog] twice, sc in next 7 sts,
** 3 sc in next st; rep from * until 19 sts remain,
rep * to ** once, 2 sc in last st, end Color C, turn.

ROW 8: Rep Row 2 using Color B.

ROW 9: Rep Row 5 using Color A
Rep Rows 2–9 for pattern.

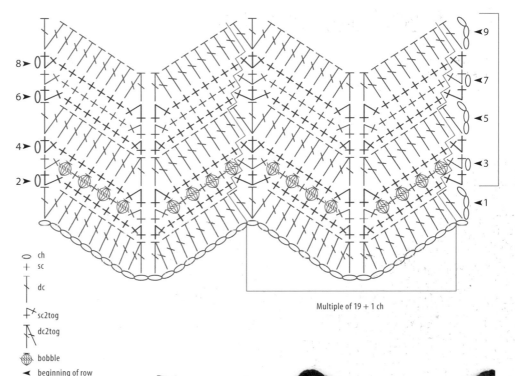

Multiple of 19 + 1 ch

○ ch
+ sc
dc
sc2tog
dc2tog
bobble
◀ beginning of row

Parisian Bobble

Follow instructions using alternative colors:

ROWS 1–2: Color A
ROW 3: Color B
ROWS 4–5: Color A
ROW 6: Color C
ROW 7: Color B
ROW 8: Color A
ROW 9: Color C

ROW 10: Rep Row 2 using Color C
ROW 11: Rep Row 3 using Color B
ROWS 12–13: Rep Rows 4–5 using Color C
ROW 14: Rep Row 6 using Color A
ROW 15: Rep Row 7 using Color B
ROW 16: Rep Row 8 using Color C
ROW 17: Rep Row 9 using Color A

■ A
□ B
■ C

Rock Pool

A
B
C
D
E

- **SKILL LEVEL:** Intermediate
- **MEASUREMENT:** One pattern repeat = 4 in. (10 cm) wide x 7 in. (18 cm) high

SPECIAL STITCH:

sc2tog: Leaving sts unfinished, sc in next 2 sts, yo and draw through all loops on hook.

dc2tog: On Row 1 only, leaving sts unfinished, dc in next 2 ch, yo and draw through all loops on hook. On all other rows, leaving sts unfinished, dc in next 2 sts, yo and draw through all loops on hook.

Bobble: Leaving sts unfinished, work 6 dc in next st, yo and draw through all loops on hook.

Method

FOUNDATION CHAIN: With Color A, ch a multiple of 15 + 1, turn foundation ch.

ROW 1: Ch 3 (counts as 1 dc), dc in 4th ch from hook, dc in next 5 ch, [dc2tog] twice, dc in next 5 ch **, 3 dc in next ch; rep from * until 15 ch remain, rep from * to **, 2 dc in last ch, end Color A, turn.

ROW 2: Join Color B, ch 3 (counts as 1 dc), dc in same place, dc in next 5 sts, [dc2tog] twice, dc in next 5 sts, * 3 dc in next st, dc in next 5 sts, [dc2tog] twice, dc in next 5 sts; rep from * until 1 st remains, 2 dc in last st, turn.

ROW 3: Ch 3 (counts as 1 dc), dc in same place, * dc in next 5 sts, [dc2tog] twice, dc in next 5 sts **, 3 dc in next st; rep from * until 15 sts remain, rep from * to ** once, 2 dc in last st, end Color B, turn.

ROW 4: Join Color C and rep Row 2.

ROW 5: Join Color D, ch 1, 2 sc in same place, * sc in next 5 sts, [sc2tog] twice, sc in next 5 sts **, 3 sc in next st; rep from * until 15 sts remain, rep from * to ** once, 2 sc in last st, end Color D, turn.

ROW 6: Join Color E, ch 1, 2 sc in same place, sc in next 5 sts, [sc2tog] twice, sc in next 5 sts, * (ch 1, Bobble, ch 1) in next st, sc in next 5 sts, [sc2tog] twice, sc in next 5 sts; rep from * until 1 st remains, 2 sc in last st, end Color F, turn.

ROW 7: Join Color D, ch 1, 2 sc in same place, sc in next 5 sts, * [sc2tog] twice, sc in next 4 sts, sc in ch-1 sp, 3 sc in next st, sc in ch-1 sp, sc in next 4 sts; rep from * until 9 sts remain, [sc2tog] twice, sc in next 5 sts, 2 sc in last st, end Color D, turn.

ROW 8: Join Color C and rep Row 2.

ROWS 9–10: Join Color B and rep Row 3, then Row 2.

ROW 11: Join Color A and rep Row 3. Rep Rows 2–11 for pattern.

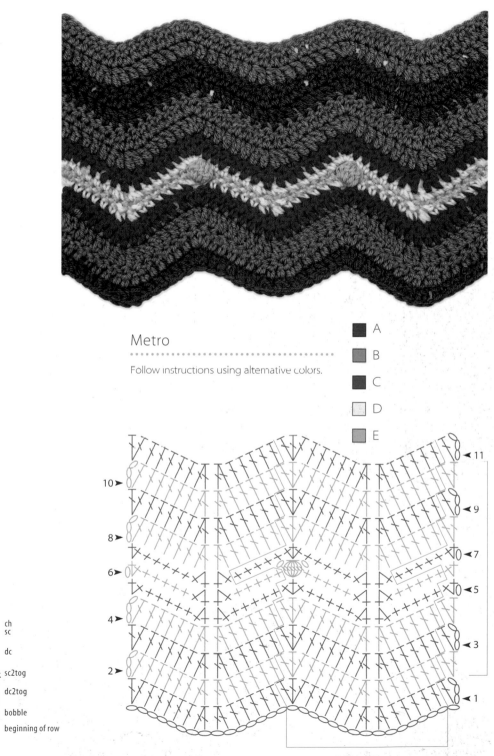

Metro

Follow instructions using alternative colors.

■	A
■	B
■	C
□	D
■	E

○ ch
+ sc
丅 dc
木 sc2tog
人 dc2tog
🌐 bobble
◄ beginning of row

Multiple of 15 + 1 ch

Roman Blinds

- **SKILL LEVEL:** Intermediate
- **MEASUREMENT:** One pattern repeat =
  5 in. (13 cm) wide x 4¼ in. (11 cm) high

SPECIAL STITCH:

dc2tog: On Row 1 only, leaving sts unfinished, dc in next 2 ch, yo and draw through all loops on hook. On all other rows, leaving sts unfinished, dc in next 2 sts, yo and draw through all loops on hook.

BPdc2tog: Leaving sts unfinished, dc around back of post of next 2 sts, yo and draw through all loops on hook.

- A
- B
- C
- D

Method

FOUNDATION CHAIN: With Color A, ch a multiple of 21 + 1, turn foundation chain.

ROW 1: Ch 3 (counts as 1 dc), 2 dc in 4th ch from hook, * dc in each of next 6 ch, [dc2tog] 4 times, dc in each of next 6 ch **, 5 dc in next ch; rep from * until 21 ch remain, rep from * to ** once, 3 dc in last ch, end Color A, turn.

ROW 2: Join Color B, ch 3 (counts as 1 dc), 2 dc in same place, BPdc in each of next 6 sts, [BPdc2tog] 4 times, BPdc in each of next 6 sts, * 5 dc in next st, BPdc in each of next 6 sts, [BPdc2tog] 4 times, BPdc in each of next 6 sts; rep from * until 1 st remains, 3 dc in last st, end Color B, turn.

ROW 3: Join Color C, ch 3 (counts as 1 dc), 2 dc in same place, dc in each of next 6 sts, [dc2tog] 4 times, dc in each of next 6 sts **, 5 dc in next st; rep from * until 21 sts remain, rep from * to ** once, 3 dc in last st, end Color C, turn.

ROW 4: Rep Row 2 using Color D.

ROW 5: Rep Rows 3 using Color A.
Rep Rows 2–5 for pattern.

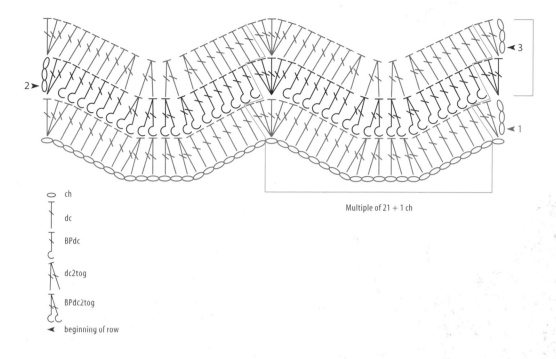

⬭	ch
†	dc
⌡	BPdc
⋀	dc2tog
⋀	BPdc2tog
◄	beginning of row

Multiple of 21 + 1 ch

Shock Wave

• **MEASUREMENT:** One pattern repeat =
5 in. (13 cm) wide x 4¼ in. (11 cm) high

Follow instructions using alternative colors:

■ A
■ B
■ C
□ D

ROW 1: Color A
ROWS 2–3: Color B
ROWS 4–5: Color C
ROWS 6–7: Color D
ROWS 8–9: Color A
Rep Rows 2–8 for pattern.

Shell Ripple

- **SKILL LEVEL:** Intermediate
- **MEASUREMENT:** One pattern repeat = 5 in. (13 cm) wide x 4¼ in. (11 cm) high

SPECIAL STITCH:

dc2tog: On Row 1 only, leaving sts unfinished, dc in next 2 ch, yo and draw through all loops on hook. On all other rows, leaving sts unfinished, dc in next 2 sts, yo and draw through all loops on hook.

Shell: 3 dc, ch 1, 3 dc in place indicated.

Method

FOUNDATION CHAIN: With Color A, ch a multiple of 8 + 9, turn foundation chain.

ROW 1: Ch 3 (counts as 1 dc), 2 dc in 4th ch from hook, * skip next 7 ch, Shell in next ch; rep from * until 8 ch remain, skip next 7 ch, 3 dc in last ch, end Color A, turn.

ROW 2: Join Color B, ch 1 and sc in same place, ch 3, * sc in 4th of skipped 7 ch, ch 7; rep from * until 3 dc of Row 1 remain, ch 3, sc in last dc of Row 1, end Color B, turn.

ROW 3: Join Color C, ch 3 (counts as 1 dc), 2 dc in same place, * Shell in next ch-1 sp working over ch 7 of Row 2; rep from * until 3 dc remain, 3 dc in last st, end Color C, turn.

ROW 4: Join Color B, ch 1 and sc in same place, ch 3, * sc in sc of Row 2, ch 7; rep until 3 dc remain, ch 3, sc in last dc, end Color B, turn.

ROW 5: Join Color D and rep Row 3, end Color D, turn.

ROW 6: Join Color B and rep Row 4, end Color B, turn.

ROW 7: Join Color C, ch 3 (counts as 1 dc), dc in same place, hold all ch-sp to the front out of the way, dc in next dc, * dc2tog, dc in next 2 dc, 3 dc over ch-7 sp of Row 6 and in ch-1 sp of Row 5, hold all ch-sp to the front, dc in next 2 sts; rep from * until 4 dc remain, dc2tog, dc in next dc, 2 dc in sc, turn.

ROW 8: Ch 3 (counts as 1 dc), dc in same place, dc in next st, dc2tog, * dc in next 2 sts, 3 dc in next st, dc in next 2 sts, dc2tog; rep until 2 sts remain, dc in next st, 2 dc in last st, turn.

ROW 9: Ch 3 (counts as 1 dc), dc in same place, dc in next st, * dc2tog, dc in next 2 sts, 3 dc in next st, dc in next 2 sts; rep from * until 4 sts remain, dc2tog, dc in next st, 2 dc in last st, turn.

ROW 10: Rep Row 8, end Color C.

ROW 11: Join Color A, ch 3 (counts as 1 dc), 2 dc in same place, * skip 6 sts, Shell in next st; rep from * until 7 sts remain, skip 6 sts, 3 dc in last st, end Color A, turn.

ROW 12: Join Color B, ch 1 and sc in same place, ch 3, sc in dc2tog of Row 10, ch 7, sc in dc2tog of Row 10; rep from * until 3 dc remain, ch 3, sc in last st, end Color B, turn.

Rep Rows 3–12 for pattern.

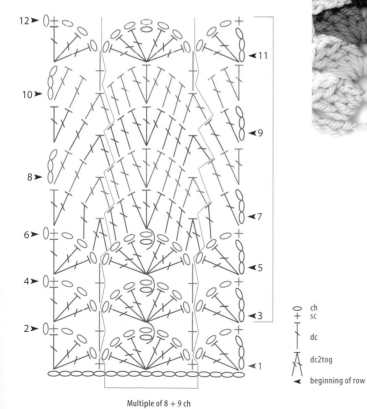

Multiple of 8 + 9 ch

+ ○   ch
+   sc
┼   dc
⅄   dc2tog
◄   beginning of row

Summer Ripple

Follow instructions using alternative colors.

ROW 1: Color A
ROW 2: Color B
ROW 3: Color C
ROW 4: Color B
ROW 5: Color D

ROW 6: Color B
ROWS 7–10: Color E
ROW 11: Color A
ROW 12: Color B

□ A
□ B
▨ C
▨ D
■ E

Bobbled Zig-zag

☐ A
◼ B
◼ C

- **SKILL LEVEL:** Intermediate
- **MEASUREMENT:** One pattern repeat =
  3½ in. (9 cm) wide x 2¾ in. (7 cm) high

SPECIAL STITCH:

sc2tog: On Row 1 only, leaving sts unfinished, sc in next 2 ch, yo and draw through all loops on hook. On all other rows, leaving sts unfinished, sc in next 2 sts, yo and draw through all loops on hook.

sc2tog tfl: Work as for sc2tog but working through the front loops.

sc2tog tbl: Work as for sc2tog but working through the back loops.

dc2tog tfl: Leaving sts unfinished and working through the front loops, dc in next 2 sts, yo and draw through all loops on hook.

Bobble: Leaving sts unfinished, work 6 tr in next st, yo and draw through all loops on hook.

Method

FOUNDATION CHAIN: With Color A, ch a multiple of 15 + 1, turn foundation chain.

ROW 1: Ch 1, 2 sc in 2nd ch from hook, * sc in each of next 5 ch, [sc2tog] twice, sc in each of next 5 ch **, 3 sc in next ch; rep from * until 15 ch remain, rep from * to ** once, 2 sc in last st, end Color A, turn.

ROW 2: Join Color B tfl, ch 1, 2 sc tfl in same place, sc tfl in each of next 5 sts, [sc2tog tfl] twice, sc tfl in each of next 5 sts, * Bobble in next st, sc tfl in each of next 5 sts, [sc2tog tfl] twice, sc tfl in each of next 5 sts; rep from * until 1 st remains, 2 sc tfl in last st, end Color B, turn.

ROW 3: Join Color A tbl, ch 1, 2 sc in same place, sc tbl in next st, * sc tbl in each of next 4 sts, [sc2tog tbl] twice, sc tbl in each of next 4 sts **, ch 1, 3 sc in Bobble, ch 1; rep from * until 14 sts remain, rep from * to ** once, sc tbl in next st, 2 sc tbl in last st, end Color A, turn.

ROW 4: Join Color C tfl, ch 3 (counts as 1 dc), dc tfl in same place, dc tfl in each of next 5 sts, [dc2tog tfl] twice, dc tfl in each of next 3 sts, * dc in ch-1 sp, dc tfl in next st, 3 dc tfl in next st, dc tfl in next st, dc in ch-1 sp, dc tfl in each of next 3 sts, [dc2tog tfl] twice, dc tfl in each of next 3 sts; rep from * until 3 sts remain, dc tfl in each of next 2 sts, 2 dc tfl in last st, end Color C, turn.

ROW 5: Join Color A tbl, ch 1, 2 sc tbl in same place, * sc tbl in each of next 5 sts, [sc2tog tbl] twice, sc tbl in each of next 5 sts **, 3 sc tbl in next st; rep from * until 15 sts remain, rep from * to ** once, 2 sc tbl in last st, end Color A, turn.

Rep Rows 2–5 for pattern.

Bloomsbury Bobble

Follow instructions using alternative colors:

ROW 1: Color A.
ROW 2: Color B.
ROW 3: Color A.
ROW 4: Color C.
ROW 5: Color B.

ROW 6: Rep Row 2 using Color A.
ROW 7: Rep Row 3 using Color B.
ROW 8: Rep Row 4 using Color C.
ROW 9: Rep Row 5 using Color A.
Rep Rows 2–9 for pattern.

■ A
□ B
■ C

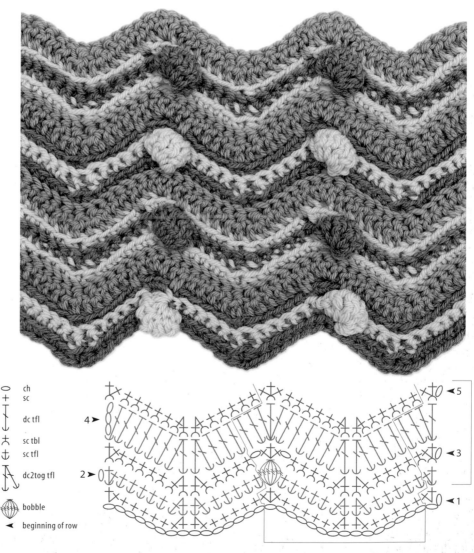

ⵔ	ch
+	sc
⟊	dc tfl
𝕏	sc tbl
𝕏	sc tfl
⋀	dc2tog tfl
⬤	bobble
◄	beginning of row

Multiple of 15 + 1 ch

PROJECT
Bag: Charleston

■ A	■ F
■ B	■ G
■ C	■ H
■ D	■ I
■ E	■ J

- **SKILL LEVEL:** Intermediate
- **MEASUREMENT:** Finished size = 12 in. (30 cm) at widest point x 9 in. (23 cm) high
- **HOOK SIZE:** E-4 (3.5 mm)
- **YARN WEIGHT:** Worsted
- **YARN AMOUNT:** A: 131 yd (120 m); B: 40 yd (37 m); C: 21 yd (19 m); D: 40 yd (37 m); E: 24 yd (22 m); F: 22 yd (20 m); G: 24 yd (22 m); H: 47 yd (43 m); I: 13 yd (12 m); J: 13 yd (12 m)
- **ADDITIONAL MATERIALS:** 7 in. (18 cm) bag frame

SPECIAL STITCH:

sc2tog: Leaving sts unfinished, sc in next 2 sts, yo and draw through all loops on hook.

sc3tog: Leaving sts unfinished, sc in next 3 sts, yo and draw through all loops on hook.

Method

HANDLE SECTION: Make 2. With Color A, ch 30.
ROW 1: Ch 1, sc in each ch across, turn.
ROW 2: Ch 1, sc in each st across, turn.
ROWS 3–7: Rep Row 2.
SURFACE CROCHET: Work rows of surface crochet across by working ch sts through gaps between sts as follows: in Row 2, Color H; in Row 3, Color J; in Row 4, Color B; in Row 5, Color D; in Row 6, Color I.

BAG

ROUND 1: Ch 1, sc in each st across one piece, then across 2nd piece, join with a sl st in the first st to form a circle—60 sts.
ROUND 2: Ch 1, sc in each st around, join with a sl st in the first st.
ROUND 3: Ch 1, sc around and increase 15 sts evenly spaced by working 2 sts in the same st, join with a sl st in the first st—75 sts.
ROUND 4: Ch 1, sc in same place, * sc in next st, hdc in next st, dc in next st, hdc in next st **, sc in next st; rep from * 13 times more, rep from * to ** once, join with a sl st in the first st, end Color A.
ROUND 5: Join Color B in next dc, ch 1, 3 sc in same place, * sc in next st, sc2tog, sc in next st **, 3 sc in next st; rep from * 13 times, rep from * to ** once, join with a sl st in the first st—90 sts.
ROUND 6: Ch 1, sc in same place, * 3 sc in next st, sc in next st, sc3tog **, sc in next st; rep from * 13 more times, rep from * to ** once, join with a sl st in the first st, end Color B.
ROUND 7: Join Color C in 2nd of 3-sc group, ch 1, 3 sc in same place, * sc in next st, sc3tog, sc in next st **, 3 sc in next st; rep from * 13 more times, rep from * to ** once, join with a sl st in the first st, end Color C.
ROUND 8: Rep Round 7 using Color D but do not end color.
ROUND 9: Rep Round 6, end Color D.
ROUND 10: Join Color E in 2nd of 3-sc group, ch 1, 5 sc in same place, * sc in next st, sc3tog, sc in next st **, 5 sc in next st; rep from * 13 times more, rep from * to ** once, join with a sl st in first st, end Color E—120 sts.
ROUND 11: Join Color F in 3rd of 5-sc group, ch 1, 3 sc in same place, * sc in each of next 2 sts, sc3tog, sc in each of next 2 sts **, 3 sc in next st; rep from * 13 times more, rep from * to ** once, join with a sl st in first st.
ROUND 12: Ch 1, sc in same place, * 3 sc in next st, sc in each of next 2 sts, sc3tog **, sc in each of next 2 sts; rep from * 13 times more, rep from * to ** once, sc in next st, join with a sl st in first st, end Color F.
ROUND 13: Rep Round 11 using Color G.
ROUNDS 14–15: Rep Rounds 11 and 12 using Color H.

ROUND 16: Join Color I in 2nd of 3-sc group, ch 1, 5 sc in same place, * sc in each of next 2 sts, sc3tog, sc in each of next 2 sts **, 5 sc in next st; rep from * 13 times more, rep from * to ** once, join with a sl st in first st, end Color I—150 sts.

ROUND 17: Join Color J in 3rd of 5-sc group, ch 1, 3 sc in same place, * sc in each of next 3 sts, sc3tog, sc in each of next 3 sts **, 3 sc in next st; rep from * 13 times more, rep from * to ** once, join with a sl st in first st.

ROUND 18: Ch 1, sc in same place, * 3 sc in next st, sc in each of next 3 sts, sc3tog **, sc in each of next 3 sts; rep from * 13 times more, rep from * to ** once, sc in each of next 2 sts, join with a sl st in first st, end Color J.

ROUND 19: Join Color E in 2nd of 3-sc group, ch 1, 3 sc in same place, * sc in each of next 3 sts, sc3tog, sc in each of next 3 sts, 3 sc in next st; rep from * 13 times more, rep from * to ** once, join with a sl st in first st, end Color E.

ROUNDS 20–21: Join Color D in 2nd of 3-sc group, ch 1 and rep Rounds 17–18.

ROUND 22: Rep Round 19 using Color G.

ROUNDS 23–24: Rep Rounds 20–21 using Color H.

ROUND 25: Rep Round 19 using Color C.

ROUNDS 26–27: Rep Rounds 20–21 using Color B.

ROUND 28: Join Color A in 2nd of 3-sc group, ch 1 and sc in same place, * sc in next st, hdc in each of next 2 sts, dc in each of next 3 sts, hdc in each of next 2 sts **, sc in each of next 2 sts; rep from * 13 more times, rep from * to ** once, sc in next st, join with a sl st in the first st, end Color A.

Weave in ends. Wash and block piece before joining the base of the bag. Once dry, join the bottom of the bag by working a row of sc using Color A.

Attach handle.

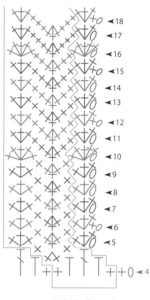

Multiple of 5 + 1 ch

○ ch
+ sc
×× sc2tog
×↑× sc3tog
◄ beginning of round

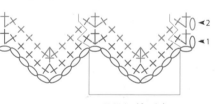

Multiple of 9 + 1 ch

Amalfi

A   B   C

- **SKILL LEVEL:** Beginner
- **MEASUREMENT:** One pattern repeat = 1½ in. (4 cm) wide x 2¾ in. (7 cm) high

FOUNDATION CHAIN: Using Color A, ch a multiple of 9 + 1, turn foundation chain.

ROW 1: Ch 1, 2 sc in 2nd ch from hook, * sc in each of next 3 ch, sc2tog, sc in each of next 3 ch **, 3 sc in next st; rep from * to last 9 ch, rep from * to ** once, 2 sc in last st, end Color A, do not turn.

ROW 2: Join Color B in first st of Row 1, ch 1, 2 sc in same place, * sc in each of next 3 sts, sc3tog, sc in each of next 3 sts **, 3 sc in next st; rep from * to last 9 sts, rep from * to ** once, 2 sc in last st, end Color B.

ROW 3: Rep Row 2 using Color A.

ROW 4: Rep Row 2 using Color C.

ROW 5: Rep Row 2 using Color B.

ROW 6: Rep Row 2 using Color C.

ROW 7: Rep Row 2 using Color A.

Rep Rows 2–7 for pattern.

PROJECT
Purse: Jitterbug

■ A
□ B
■ C
□ D
■ E
□ F

- **SKILL LEVEL:** Intermediate
- **MEASUREMENT:** Finished size = 5 in. (13 cm) at widest point x 4 in. (10 cm) high
- **HOOK SIZE:** E-4 (3.5 mm)
- **YARN WEIGHT:** Worsted
- **YARN AMOUNT:** A: 304 yd (278 m); B: 8 yd (7 m); C: 10 ft (3 m); D: 13 ft (4 m); E; 13 ft (4 m); F: 13 ft (4 m)
- **ADDITIONAL MATERIALS:** 3 in. (7.5 cm) purse frame

SPECIAL STITCH:

sc2tog: Leaving sts unfinished, sc in next 2 sts, yo and draw through all loops on hook.
sc3tog: Leaving sts unfinished, sc in next 3 sts, yo and draw through all loops on hook.

Method

HANDLE SECTION Make 2.
With Color A, ch 13.
ROW 1: Ch 1, sc in each ch across, turn—13 sts.
ROW 2: Ch 1, sc in each st across, turn.
ROWS 3–6: Rep Row 2.

PURSE

ROUND 1: Ch 1, sc in each st across one piece, then across 2nd piece, join with a sl st in first st to form a circle—26 sts.
ROUND 2: Ch 1, sc around and increase 4 sts evenly spaced by working 2 sts in the same st, join with a sl st in the first st—30 sts.
ROUND 3: Ch 1, sc in same place, * sc in next st, hdc in next st, dc in next st, hdc in next st **, sc in next st; rep from * 4 times more, rep from * to ** once, join with a sl st to first st made, end Color A.
ROUND 4: Join Color B in next dc, ch 1, 3 sc in same place, * sc in next st, sc2tog, sc in next st **, 3 sc in next st; rep from * 4 more times, rep from * to ** once, join with a sl st in first st, end Color B—36 sts.
ROUND 5: Join Color C in 2nd st of 3-sc group, ch 1, 3 sc in same place, * sc in next st, sc3tog, sc in next st **, 3 sc in next st; rep

from * 4 more times, rep from * to ** once, join with a sl st in the first st, end Color C.
ROUND 6: Join Color D in 2nd st of 3-sc group, ch 1, 5 sc in same place, * sc in next st, sc3tog, sc in next st **, 5 sc in next st; rep from * 4 more times, rep from * to ** once, join with a sl st in first st, end Color D—48 sts.
ROUND 7: Join Color E in 3rd st of 5-sc group, ch 1, 3 sc in same place, * sc in each of next 2 sts, sc3tog, sc in each of next 2 sts **, 3 sc in next st; rep from * 4 more times, rep from * to ** once, join with a sl st in first st, end Color E.
ROUND 8: Join Color F in 2nd st of 3-sc group, ch 1, 3 sc in same place, * sc in each of next 2 sts, sc3tog, sc in each of next 2 sts **, 3 sc in next st; rep from * 4 more times, rep from * to ** once, join with a sl st in first st, end Color F.
ROUND 9: Join Color B in 2nd st of 3-sc group, ch 1, 5 sc in same place, * sc in each of next 2 sts, sc3tog, sc in each of next 2 sts **, 5 sc in next st; rep from * 4 times more, rep from * to ** once, join with a sl st in first st, end Color B—60 sts.
ROUND 10: Join Color A in 3rd st of 5-sc group, ch 1, sc in same place, * sc in next st, hdc in each of next 2 sts, dc in each of next 3 sts, hdc in each of next 2 sts **, sc in each of next 2 sts; rep from * 4 more times, rep from * to ** once, sc in next st, join with a sl st in first st, end Color A.

Weave in ends. Wash and block piece before joining the base of the bag. Once dry, join the bottom of the bag by working a row of sc using Color A.

Attach handle.

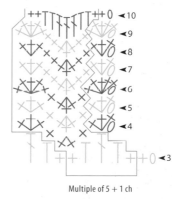

Multiple of 5 + 1 ch

○ ch
+ sc
✕✕ sc2tog
✕⋔ sc3tog
◄ beginning of round

Aspen

- **SKILL LEVEL:** Intermediate
- **MEASUREMENT:** One pattern repeat = 4¾ in. (12 cm) wide x 6 in. (15 cm) high

A
B
C
D
E

SPECIAL STITCH:

dc2tog: On Row 1 only, leaving sts unfinished, dc in next ch, skip 2 ch, dc in next ch, yo and draw through all loops on hook.
On all other rows, leaving sts unfinished, dc in next st, skip 1 st, dc in next st, yo and draw through all loops on hook.

sc2tog: Leaving sts unfinished, sc in next st, skip 1 st, sc in next st, yo and draw through all loops on hook.

Cross Stitch: Skip 1 st, dc in next st, working in front of st just made dc in skipped st.

Method

FOUNDATION CHAIN: With Color A, ch a multiple of 21 + 1, turn foundation chain.

ROW 1: Ch 3 (counts as 1 dc), dc in 4th ch from hook, * work Cross Stitch in next 8 ch (four cross sts made), dc2tog, work Cross Stitch in next 8 ch (four cross sts made) **, 3 dc in next st; rep from * until 21 ch remain, rep from * to ** once, 2 dc in last st, end Color A, turn.

ROW 2: Join Color B, ch 1, 2 sc in same place, sc in each of next 8 sts, sc2tog, sc in each of next 8 sts, * 3 sc in next st, sc in each of next 8 sts, sc2tog, sc in each of next 8 sts; rep from * until 1 st remains, 2 sc in last st, end Color B, turn.

ROW 3: Join Color C, ch 3 (counts as 1 dc), dc in same place, * work Cross Stitch in next 8 sts, dc2tog, work Cross Stitch in next 8 sts **, 3 dc in next st; rep from * until 20 sts remain, rep from * to ** once, 2 dc in last st, end Color C, turn.

ROW 4: Rep Row 2 using Color D.
ROW 5: Rep Row 3 using Color E.
ROW 6: Rep Row 2 using Color A.
ROW 7: Rep Row 3 using Color B.
ROW 8: Rep Row 2 using Color C.
ROW 9: Rep Row 3 using Color D.
ROW 10: Rep Row 2 using Color E.
ROW 11: Rep Row 3 using Color A.
Rep Rows 2–11 for pattern.

Plum Strata

Follow instructions using alternative colors:

ROW 1: Color A
ROW 2: Color B
ROW 3: Color C
ROW 4: Color D
ROW 5: Color A
Rep Rows 2–5 for pattern.

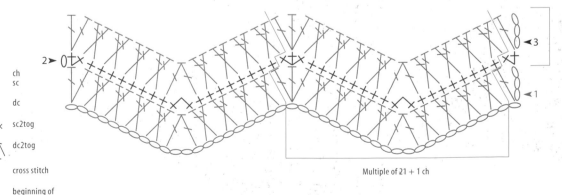

○	ch
+	sc
┬	dc
⋏	sc2tog
⋏	dc2tog
✕	cross stitch
◄	beginning of row

Multiple of 21 + 1 ch

Pink Haze

- **SKILL LEVEL:** Intermediate
- **MEASUREMENT:** One pattern repeat =
  4¾ in. (12 cm) wide x 3¼ in. (8 cm) high

SPECIAL STITCH:

dc2tog: On Row 1 only, leaving sts unfinished, dc in next ch, skip 1 ch, dc in next ch, yo and draw through all loops on hook.
On all other rows, leaving sts unfinished, dc in next st, skip 1 st, dc in next st, yo and draw through all loops on hook.

■ A
■ B
■ C
□ D

Method

FOUNDATION CHAIN: With Color A, ch a multiple of 22 + 1, turn foundation chain.

ROW 1: Ch 3 (counts as 1 dc), dc in 4th ch from hook, * dc in each of next 9 ch, dc2tog, dc in each of next 9 ch **, (dc, ch 1, dc) in next ch; rep from * until 22 ch remain, rep from * to ** once, 2 dc in last ch, end Color A, turn.

ROW 2: Join Color B, ch 3 (counts as 1 dc), dc in same place, [BPdc in next st, FPdc in next st] 4 times, BPdc in next st, dc2tog, [BPdc in next st, FPdc in next st] 4 times, BPdc in next st, * (dc, ch 1, dc) in ch-sp, [BPdc in next st, FPdc in next st] 4 times, BPdc in next st, dc2tog, [BPdc in next st, FPdc in next st] 4 times, BPdc in next st; rep from * until 1 st remains, 2 dc in last st, end Color B, turn.

ROW 3: Join Color C, ch 3 (counts as 1 dc), dc in same place, * [BPdc in next st, FPdc in next st] 4 times, BPdc in next st, dc2tog, [BPdc in next st, FPdc in next st] 4 times, BPdc in next st **, (dc, ch 1, dc) in ch-sp; rep from * until 22 sts remain, rep from * to ** once, 2 dc in last st, end Color C, turn.

ROW 4: Rep Row 2 using Color D.

ROW 5: Rep Row 3 using Color A.
Rep Rows 2–5 for pattern.

Mulberry Whip

Follow instructions using alternative colors:

ROW 1: Color A

ROW 2: Color B

ROW 3: Color C

ROW 4: Color B

ROW 5: Color A
Rep Rows 2–5 for pattern.

■ A
■ B
■ C

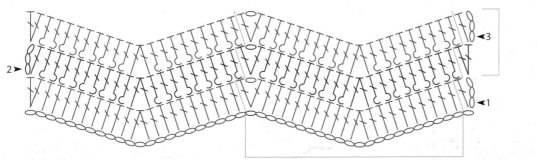

ch
sc
dc
BPdc
FPdc
dc2tog
beginning of row

Multiple of 22 + 1 ch

Shinto

A

B

C

- **SKILL LEVEL:** Intermediate
- **MEASUREMENT:** One pattern repeat = 3¼ in. (8 cm) wide x 5 in. (13 cm) high

SPECIAL STITCH:

sc2tog: Leaving sts unfinished, sc in next 2 sts, yo and draw through all loops on hook.

sc2tog over next 3 sts: Leaving sts unfinished, sc in next st, skip 1 st, sc in next st, yo and draw through all loops on hook.

Beg scdec: Leaving sts unfinished, sc in next 2 sts, yo and draw through all loops on hook.

End scdec: Leaving sts unfinished, sc in next 2 sts, yo and draw through all loops on hook.

Method

FOUNDATION CHAIN: With Color A, ch a multiple of 8 + 1, turn foundation chain.

ROW 1: Ch 1 and sc in 2nd ch from hook, skip 3 ch, 10 dc in next ch, skip 3 ch, sc in next ch; rep from * to last 8 ch, skip 3 ch, 10 dc in next ch, skip 3 ch, sc in last ch, end Color A, turn.

ROW 2: Join Color B, ch 1 and Beg sc dec, sc in each of next 3 sts, [2 sc in next st] twice, sc in each of next 3 sts, * sc2tog over 3 sts, sc in each of next 3 sts, [2 sc in next st] twice, sc in each of next 3 sts; rep from * to last 2 sts, end scdec in last 2 sts, turn.

ROWS 3–4: Rep Row 2, turn, end Color B at end of Row 4.

ROW 5: Join Color A, ch 3 (counts as 1 dc), 4 dc in same place, skip 4 sts, * sc2tog, skip 4 sts, 10 dc in next st, skip 4 sts; rep from * to last 7 sts, sc2tog, skip 4 sts, 5 dc in last st, end Color A, turn.

ROW 6: Join Color C, ch 1 and 2 sc in same place, sc in each of next 3 sts, sc2tog over 3 sts, sc in each of next 3 sts, * [2 sc in next st] twice, sc in each of next 3 sts, sc2tog over 3 sts, sc in each of next 3 sts; rep from * to last st, 2 sc in last st, turn.

ROWS 7–8: Rep Row 6, turn, end Color C at end of Row 8.

ROW 9: Join Color A, ch 1 and sc in same place, * skip 4 sts, 10 dc in next st, skip 4 sts **, sc2tog; rep from * to last 10 sts, rep from * to ** once, sc in last st, end Color A, turn. Rep Rows 2–9 for pattern.

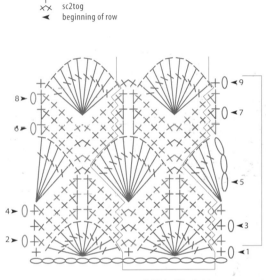

○	ch
+	sc
╪	dc
××	sc2tog
◄	beginning of row

Multiple of 8 + 1 ch

Kyoto

Follow instructions using alternative colors:

ROW 1: Color A
ROWS 2–4: Color B
ROW 5: Color C
ROWS 6–8: Color B
ROW 9: Color D
Repeat Rows 2–9 for pattern, alternating Colors A, C, and D in Rows 5 and 9.

■ A
■ B
■ C
■ D

Confetti

- **SKILL LEVEL:** Intermediate
- **MEASUREMENT:** One pattern repeat =
  6 in. (15 cm) wide x 5½ in. (14 cm) high

☐ A
■ B
☐ C
☐ D
☐ E

SPECIAL STITCH:

sc2tog: Leaving sts unfinished, sc in next 2 sts or ch, yo and draw through all loops on hook.
dc2tog: Leaving sts unfinished, dc in next 2 sts or ch, yo and draw through all loops on hook.
Flower: Ch 5, sl st in first ch, [ch 4, sl st in first ch of beginning ch-5] 5 times.

Method

FOUNDATION CHAIN: With Color A, ch a multiple of 24, turn foundation chain.

ROW 1: Ch 3 (counts as 1 dc), dc in 4th ch from hook, * dc in each of next 9 ch, [dc2tog] twice, dc in each of next 9 ch **, [2 dc in next ch] twice; rep from * to last 23 ch, rep from * to ** once, 2 dc in last st, do not turn.

ROW 2: Join Color B in first st of last row, ch 1 and 2 sc in same place, * sc in each of next 9 sts, sc2tog, Flower, sc2tog, sc in each of next 9 sts **, 2 sc in next st, Flower, 2 sc in next st; rep from * to last 23 sts, rep from * to ** once, 2 sc in last st, end Color B, do not turn.

ROW 3: Join Color A in first st of last row, ch 3 (counts as 1 dc), dc in same place, * dc in each of next 9 sts, [dc2tog] twice, dc in each of next 9 sts **, [2 dc in next st] twice; rep from * to last 23 sts, rep from * to ** once, 2 dc in last st, end Color A, do not turn.

ROW 4: Join Color C in first st of last row, ch 1 and 2 sc in same place, * sc in each of next 5 sts, Flower, sc in each of next 4 sts, [sc2tog] twice, sc in each of next 4 sts, Flower, sc in each of next 5 sts **, [2 sc in next st] twice; rep from * to last 23 sts, rep from * to ** once, 2 sc in last st, end Color C, do not turn.

ROW 5: Join Color A and rep Row 3.

ROW 6: Join Color D and rep Row 2.

ROW 7: Join Color A and rep Row 3.

ROW 8: Join Color E and rep Row 4.

ROW 9: Join Color A and rep Row 3.
Rep Rows 2–9 for pattern.

Flower Meadow

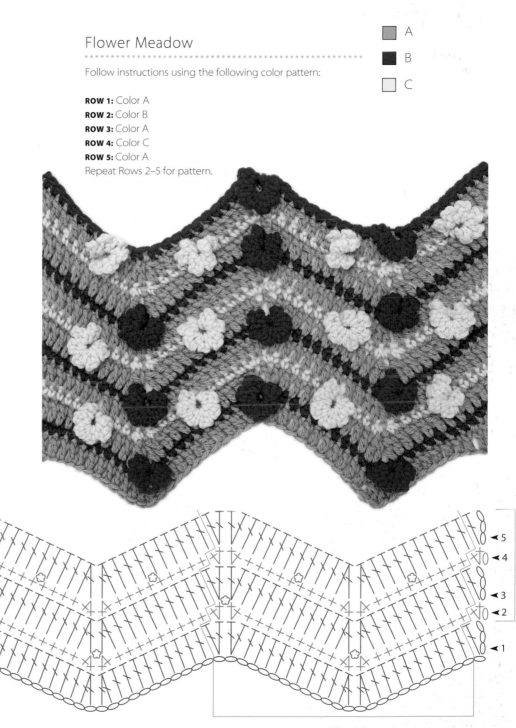

	A
	B
	C

Follow instructions using the following color pattern:

ROW 1: Color A
ROW 2: Color B
ROW 3: Color A
ROW 4: Color C
ROW 5: Color A
Repeat Rows 2–5 for pattern.

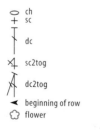

○ ch
+ sc
↑ dc
✕ sc2tog
⋔ dc2tog
◀ beginning of row
✿ flower

Multiple of 24 ch

Kaleidoscope

- **SKILL LEVEL:** Intermediate
- **MEASUREMENT:** One pattern repeat = 9 in. (23 cm) wide x 9 in. (23 cm) high

SPECIAL STITCH:

sc3tog: Leaving sts unfinished, sc in next 3 sts, yo and draw through all loops on hook.
thb: Work through the horizontal bar at the back of each st.

☐ A
■ B
☐ C
☐ D
■ E

Method

FOUNDATION RING: With Color A, make a Magic Ring.

ROUND 1: Ch 1, 8 sc into ring, join with sl st in beginning-ch, end Color A—8 sts.

ROUND 2: Join Color B, ch 1, 2 sc in each st around, join with sl st in beginning-ch, end Color B—16 sts.

ROUND 3: Join Color C, ch 1, [2 sc in next st, sc in next st] 8 times, join with sl st in beginning-ch, end Color C—24 sts.

ROUND 4: Join Color D, ch 1, [sc in each of next 2 sts, 2 sc in next st] 8 times, join with sl st in beginning-ch, end Color D—32 sts.

ROUND 5: Join Color E, ch 1, [sc in next st, hdc in next st, 3 dc in next st, hdc in next st] 8 times, join with sl st in beginning-ch, end Color E—40 sts.

ROUND 6: Join Color A through horizontal bar of 2nd st of 3-dc group, ch 1 and 5 sc thb in same place, * sc thb in next st, sc3tog thb, sc thb in next st **, 5 sc thb in next st; rep from * 6 times, rep from * to ** once, join with sl st in beginning ch, end Color A.

ROUND 7: Join Color B in 3rd st of 5 sc group, ch 1 and 5 sc in same place, * sc in each st to 1 st before decrease, sc3tog, sc in each st to 2nd st of 5-sc group **, 5 sc in next st; repeat from * 6 times, rep from * to ** once, join with sl st in beginning-ch, end Color B.

ROUNDS 8–9: Repeat Round 7 using Color C, then Color D.

ROUND 10: Join Color E in 3rd st of 5-sc group, ch 3 (counts as 1 dc), 4 dc in same place, * dc in each st to 1 st before decrease, sc3tog, dc in each st to 2nd st of next 5-sc group **, 5 dc in next st; rep from * 5 times, rep from * to ** once, join with sl st in top of beginning-ch, end Color E.

ROUND 11: Join Color A thb in 3rd st of 5-dc group, ch 1 and 5 sc thb in same place, * sc thb in each st to 1 st before decrease, sc3tog thb, sc thb in each st to 2nd st of next 5-dc group **, 5 sc thb in next st; rep from * 6 times, rep from * to ** once, join with sl st in beginning-ch, end Color A.

Rep Rounds 7–11 for pattern.

○	ch
•	sl st
+	sc
†	dc
⨯	sc3tog
+	sc thb
⋏	5 sc thb
◄	beginning of round

Springtime

A
B
C

Follow instructions using alternative colors.

ROUND 1: Color A
ROUND 2: Color B
ROUND 3: Color A
ROUND 4: Color B
ROUND 5: Color C
ROUND 6: Color A
ROUND 7: Color B
ROUND 8: Color A
ROUND 9: Color B
ROUND 10: Color C
ROUND 11: Color A
Rep Rounds 7–11 for pattern.

Harvest

- **SKILL LEVEL:** Intermediate
- **MEASUREMENT:** One pattern repeat =
  3½ in. (9 cm) wide x 4¾ in. (12 cm) high

SPECIAL STITCH:

sc3tog: Leaving sts unfinished, sc in next 3 sts, yo and draw through all loops on hook.

dc3tog: Leaving sts unfinished, dc in next 3 sts or ch, yo and draw through all loops on hook.

dc5tog: Leaving sts unfinished, dc in next 5 sts, yo and draw through all loops on hook.

A
B
C
D

Method

FOUNDATION CHAIN: With Color A, ch a multiple of 12 + 1, turn foundation chain.

ROW 1: Ch 3 (counts as 1 dc), dc in 4th ch from hook, * dc in each of next 4 ch, dc3tog, dc in each of next 4 ch **, 3 dc in next ch; rep from * to last 12 ch, rep from * to ** once, 2 dc in last st, turn.

ROW 2: Ch 3 (counts as 1 dc), dc in same place, dc in each of next 4 sts, dc3tog, dc in each of next 4 sts, * 3 dc in next st, dc in each of next 4 sts, dc3tog, dc in each of next 4 sts; rep from * to last st, 2 dc in last st, end Color A, turn.

ROW 3: Join Color B, ch 1, 2 sc in same place, * sc in each of next 4 sts, sc3tog, sc in each of next 4 sts **, 3 sc in next st; rep from * to last 12 sts, rep from * to ** once, 2 sc in last st, end Color B, turn.

ROW 4: Join Color C, ch 1, 2 sc in same place, [tr in next st, sc in next st] 5 times, tr in next st, * 3 sc in next st, [tr in next st, sc in next st] 5 times, tr in next st; rep from * to last st, 2 sc in last st, end Color C, turn.

ROW 5: Join Color D, ch 3 (counts as 1 dc), dc in same place, * dc in each of next 4 sts, dc5tog, dc in each of next 4 sts **, 3 dc in next st; rep from * to last 14 sts, rep from * to ** once, 2 dc in last st, turn.

ROW 6: Ch 3 (counts as 1 dc), dc in same place, dc in each of next 4 sts, dc3tog, dc in each of next 4 sts, * 3 dc in next st, dc in each of next 4 sts, dc3tog, dc in each of next 4 sts; rep from * to last st, 2 dc in last st, end Color D, turn.

Rep Rows 3–6 for pattern, alternating Colors A and D for each rep of Rows 5 and 6.

Bonfire

Follow instructions using alternative colors.

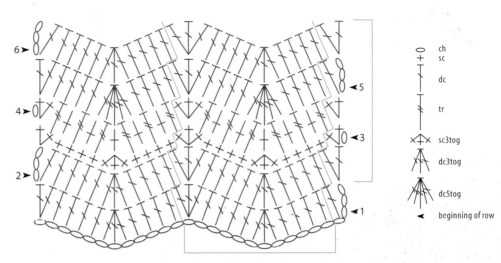

Multiple of 12 + 1 ch

○	ch
+	sc
†	dc
‡	tr
✕	sc3tog
↟	dc3tog
↟	dc5tog
◄	beginning of row

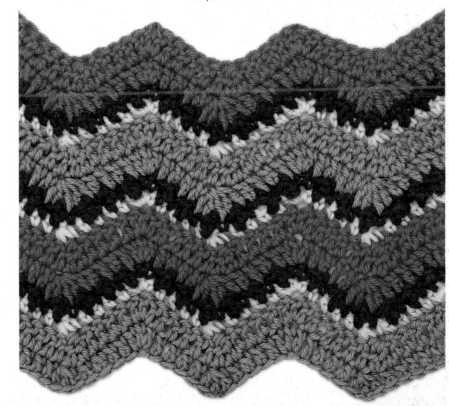

■ A
□ B
■ C
■ D

Ocean Swell

□ A

□ B

■ C

- **SKILL LEVEL:** Intermediate
- **MEASUREMENT:** One pattern repeat = 7½ in. (19 cm) wide x 5 in. (13 cm) high

SPECIAL STITCH:

Bead Stitch: Dc into place indicated, work a hdc cluster [(yo, insert hook under post, yo and draw up a loop) 3 times, yo and draw through all loops on hook] around the post of the dc.

Method

FOUNDATION CHAIN: With Color A, ch a multiple of 29 + 25, turn foundation chain.

ROW 1: Ch 3 (counts as 1 dc), 3 dc in 4th ch from hook, * dc in each of next 7 ch, [skip 1 ch, dc in next st] 5 times, dc in each of next 6 ch **, ch 1, skip 1 ch, [Bead Stitch in next st, ch 1] 4 times, skip 1 ch; rep from * to last 24 ch, rep from * to ** once, 4 dc in last st, end Color A, do not turn.

ROW 2: Join Color B in first st of last row, ch 3 (counts as 1 dc), 3 dc in same place, dc in each of next 2 sts, * dc in each of next 5 sts, [skip 1 st, dc in next st] 5 times, dc in each of next 4 sts **, dc in ch-sp, dc in Bead Stitch, ch 1, Bead Stitch in ch-sp, ch 1, (Bead Stitch, ch 1, Bead Stitch) in next ch-sp, ch 1, Bead Stitch in next ch-sp, ch 1, dc in Bead Stitch, dc in ch-sp; rep from * to last 22 sts, rep from * to ** once, dc in each of next 2 sts, 4 dc in last st, end Color B, do not turn.

ROW 3: Repeat Row 2 using Color C.

ROW 4: Repeat Row 2 using Color B.

ROW 5: Repeat Row 2 using Color A.
Repeat Rows 2–5 for pattern.

Blue Ridge

Follow instructions using alternative colors, and changing color every row.

☐	A
☐	B
■	C

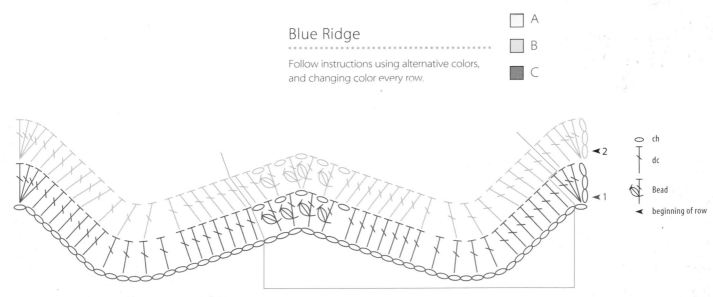

◯	ch
⊢	dc
⬦	Bead
◄	beginning of row

Multiple of 29 + 25 ch

Orion's Belt

- **SKILL LEVEL:** Intermediate
- **MEASUREMENT:** One pattern repeat = 11¾ in. (30 cm) wide x 6 in. (15 cm) high

SPECIAL STITCH:

sc3tog: Leaving sts unfinished, sc in next 3 sts, yo and draw through all loops on hook.

dc2tog: Leaving sts unfinished, dc in next st, skip 1 st, dc in next st, yo and draw through all loops on hook.

☐ A
■ B
■ C
☐ D

Method

FOUNDATION CHAIN: With Color A, ch 19.

ROUND 1: Ch 1, sc in 2nd ch from hook, [hdc in next ch, dc in next ch, (2 dc, ch 1, 2 dc) in next ch, dc in next ch, hdc in next ch, sc in next ch] 3 times, ch 1, turn work with remaining edge of foundation ch up, sc in next ch, [hdc in next ch, dc in next ch, (2 dc, ch 1, 2 dc) in next ch, dc in next ch, hdc in next ch, sc in next ch] 3 times, ch 1, join with sl st in beginning-ch, end Color A.

ROUND 2: Join Color B in ch-1 sp at end of last round, ch 1 and 3 sc in same place, *sc in each st to ch-sp, [3 sc in ch-sp, sc in each of next 3 sts, sc3tog, sc in each of next 3 sts] twice, 3 sc in ch-sp **, sc in each st to ch-sp, 3 sc in ch sp; rep from * to ** once, sc in each st to end of rnd, join with sl st in beginning-ch, end Color B.

ROUND 3: Join Color C in 2nd st of 3-sc group at end of last rnd, ch 3 (counts as 1 dc), (dc, ch 1, 2 dc) in same place, * dc in each st to 2nd st of 3-sc group, [(2 dc, ch 2, 2 dc) in next st, dc in each st to 1 st before decrease, dc2tog, dc in each st to 2nd st of 3-sc group] twice, (2 dc, ch 1, 2 dc) in next st **, dc in each st to 2nd st of 3-sc group, (2 dc, ch 1, 2 dc) in next st; rep from * to ** once more, dc in each st to end of rnd, join with sl st in beginning ch.

ROUND 4: Join Color D in ch-1 sp at end of last rnd, ch 1 and 3 sc in same place, * sc in each st to next ch-sp, [3 sc in ch-sp, sc in each st to 1 st before decrease, sc3tog, sc in each st to ch-sp] twice, 3 sc in ch-sp **, sc in each st to next ch sp, 3 sc in ch-sp, rep from * to ** once, sc in each st to end of rnd, join with sl st in beginning-ch, end Color D. Repeat Rounds 3–4, changing colors on each round.

⬭	ch
•	sl st
+	sc
┬	hdc
┤	dc
⤬	sc3tog
⋀	dc2tog
◄	beginning of round

Big Dipper

Follow instructions using alternative colors.

◻	A
◻	B
◼	C
◼	D

Strawberry Mint

- **SKILL LEVEL:** Intermediate
- **MEASUREMENT:** One pattern repeat =
  4 in. (10 cm) wide x 6¼ in. (16 cm) high

SPECIAL STITCH:

dc2tog: Leaving sts unfinished, dc in next 2 ch or sts, yo and draw through all loops on hook.

BPdc2tog: Leaving sts unfinished, BPdc in next 2 sts, yo and draw through all loops on hook.

thb: Work through the horizontal bar at the back of each st.

A
B
C

Method

FOUNDATION CHAIN: With Color A, ch a multiple of 17 + 1, turn foundation chain.

ROW 1: Ch 3 (counts as 1 dc), 2 dc in 4th ch from hook, * dc in each of next 4 ch, skip next ch, [dc2tog] 4 times, skip next ch, dc in each of next 4 ch **, (2 dc, ch 1, 2 dc) in next ch; rep from * to last 17 ch, rep from * to ** once, 3 dc in last ch, end Color A, do not turn.

ROW 2: Join Color B in first st of last row, ch 3 (counts as 1 dc), 2 dc in same place, dc thb in each of next 4 sts, [dc2tog thb] 4 times, dc thb in each of next 4 sts **, (2 dc, ch 1, 2 dc) in ch-sp; rep from * to last 17 sts, rep from * to ** once, 3 dc in last st, end Color B, do not turn.

ROW 3: Join Color C in first st of last row, and repeat Row 2.

ROW 4: Join Color A in first st of last row, and repeat Row 2.

ROW 5: Join Color B in first st of last row, ch 3 (counts as 1 dc), 2 dc in same place, BPdc in each of next 4 sts, [BPdc2tog] 4 times, BPdc in each of next 4 sts **, (2 dc, ch 1, 2 dc) in ch-sp; rep from * to last 17 sts, rep from * to ** once, 3 dc in last st, end Color B, do not turn.

ROW 6: Join Color C in first st of last row, and repeat Row 5.

ROW 7: Join Color A in first st of last row, and repeat Row 5.

ROW 8: Join Color B in first st of last row, ch 3 (counts as 1 dc), 2 dc in same place, dc thb in each of next 4 sts, [dc2tog thb] 4 times, dc thb in each of next 4 sts **, (2 dc, ch 1, 2 dc) in ch-sp; rep from * to last 17 sts, rep from * to ** once, 3 dc in last st, end Color B, do not turn.

Repeat Rows 3–8 for pattern.

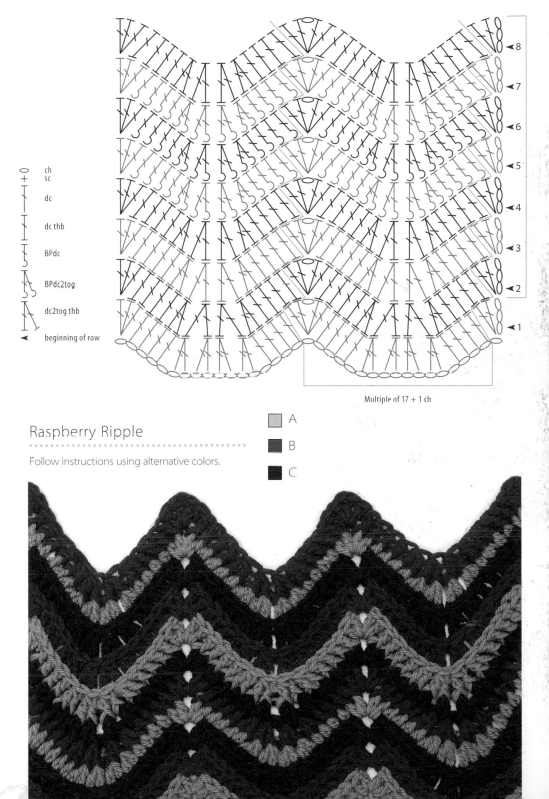

$+$ o	ch
	sc
	dc
	dc thb
	BPdc
	BPdc2tog
	dc2tog thb
◄	beginning of row

Multiple of 17 + 1 ch

Raspberry Ripple

Follow instructions using alternative colors.

■ A
■ B
■ C

Tulips

A

B

C

- **SKILL LEVEL:** Intermediate
- **MEASUREMENT:** One pattern repeat =
  5 in. (13 cm) wide x 3½ in. (9 cm) high

SPECIAL STITCH:

dc-dec: On Row 1 only, leaving sts unfinished, dc in next ch, skip 2 ch, dc in next ch, yo and draw through all loops on hook. On all other rows, leaving sts unfinished, dc in next ch, skip 1 st, dc in next ch, yo and draw through all loops on hook.

Cluster: Leaving sts unfinished, work 3 dc in same st, yo and draw through all loops on hook.

V Stitch: (dc, ch 1, dc) in same space.

thb: Work through the horizontal bar at the back of each st.

Method

FOUNDATION CHAIN: With Color A, ch a multiple of 19 + 1, turn foundation chain.

ROW 1: Ch 3 (counts as 1 dc), dc in 4th ch from hook, * [ch 1, skip 1 ch, Cluster in next ch] 3 times, ch 1, skip 1 ch, dc-dec, [ch 1, skip 1 ch, Cluster in next ch] 3 times, ch 1, skip 1 ch **, V Stitch in next ch; rep from * to last 19 ch, rep from * to ** once, 2 dc in last ch, end Color A, turn.

ROW 2: Join Color B, ch 3 (counts as 1 dc), dc in same place, V Stitch in each of next 3 ch-sp, ch 1, dc-dec, ch 1, * V Stitch in each of next 7 ch-sp, ch 1, dc-dec, ch 1; rep from * to last 5 sts (not including ch-sp), V Stitch in each of next 3 ch-sp, skip 1 st, 2 dc in last st, end Color B, turn.

ROW 3: Join Color C, ch 3 (counts as 1 dc), dc in same place, * [ch 1, Cluster in next ch-sp] 3 times, ch 1, dc-dec, ch 1, [Cluster in next ch-sp, ch 1] 3 times **, V Stitch in next ch-sp; rep from * to last 16 sts, rep from * to ** once, skip 2 sts, 2 dc in last st, end Color C, turn.

ROW 4: Repeat Row 2 using Color B.

ROW 5: Repeat Row 3 using Color A.
Repeat Rows 2–5 for pattern.

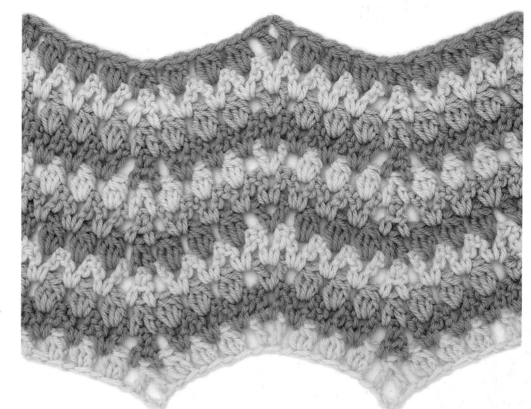

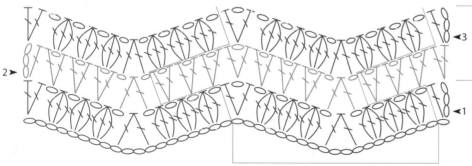

Multiple of 19 + 1 ch

ch

dc

cluster

dc2tog

v stitch

◄ beginning of row

Easter

· ·

· **MEASUREMENT:** One repeat = 5 in. (13 cm) wide x 2¾ in. (7 cm) high

Follow instructions using alternative colors:

ROW 1: Color A
ROW 2: Color B
ROW 3: Color C
ROW 4: Color A
Repeat Rows 2–4 for pattern.

☐ A
▨ B
▨ C

Ferris Wheel

- **SKILL LEVEL:** Intermediate
- **MEASUREMENT:** One pattern repeat = 9¾ in. (25 cm) wide x 9¾ in. (25 cm) high

SPECIAL STITCH:

sc2tog: Leaving sts unfinished, sc in next st, skip 1 st, sc in next st, yo and draw through all loops on hook.

dc2tog: Leaving sts unfinished, dc in next st, skip 1 st, dc in next st, yo and draw through all loops on hook.

thb: Work through the horizontal bar at the back of each st.

Method

FOUNDATION CHAIN: With Color A, ch 8, join with sl st in first ch to form a ring.

ROUND 1: Ch 1, 12 sc into ring, join with sl st in top of beginning-ch.

ROUND 2: Ch 5 (counts as 1 dc, ch 2), [dc in next st, ch 2] 11 times, join with sl st in 3rd ch of beginning-ch.

ROUND 3: Ch 3 (counts as 1 dc), dc in same place, [sc2tog in this ch-sp and next ch-sp, 3 dc in same ch-sp] 11 times, sc2tog in same ch-sp and first ch-sp, join with sl st in top of beginning-ch, end Color A.

ROUND 4: Join Color B thb, ch 3 (counts as 1 dc), 4 dc thb in same place, [sc2tog thb, 5 dc thb in next st] 11 times, sc2tog thb, join with sl st in top of beginning-ch, end Color B.

ROUND 5: Join Color C thb of 3rd st of 5-dc group, ch 3 (counts as 1 dc), 4 dc thb in same place, [dc thb in next st, sc2tog thb, dc thb in next st, 5 dc thb in next st] 11 times, dc thb in next st, sc2tog thb, dc thb in next st, join with sl st in top of beginning-ch, end Color C.

ROUND 6: Join Color A tbh of 3rd st of 5-dc group, ch 3 (counts as 1 dc), (dc, ch 1, 2 dc) in same place, [dc thb in each st to 1 st before decrease, sc2tog thb, dc thb in each st to 3rd st of 5-dc group, (2 dc, ch 1, 2 dc) tbh in next st] 11 times, dc thb in each st to 1 st before decrease, sc2tog thb, dc thb in each st to end of round, join with sl st in top of beginning-ch, end Color A.

ROUND 7: Join Color B in ch-sp, ch 3 (counts as 1 dc), (dc, ch 2, 2 dc) in same place, [dc in each st to 1 st before decrease, dc2tog, dc in each st to ch-sp, (2 dc, ch 2, 2 dc) in ch-sp] 11 times, dc in each st to 1 st before decrease, dc2tog, dc in each st to end of round, join with sl st in top of beginning-ch, end Color B.

Repeat Round 7, changing color for each round.

Rosette

· ·

Follow instructions using alternative colors.

⬭	ch
·	sl st
+	sc
±	sc thb
⊤	dc
⊥	dc thb
⋏	sc2tog
⋔	dc2tog
⋏	sc2tog thb
◄	beginning of round

☐	A
■	B
☐	C

PROJECT
Afghan: Retro Rose

A
B
C
D
E

- **SKILL LEVEL:** Intermediate
- **MEASUREMENT:** Finished size = 46 in. (117 cm) diameter point to point
- **HOOK SIZE:** J-10 (6 mm)
- **YARN WEIGHT:** Worsted
- **YARN AMOUNT:** A: 201 yd (184 m); B: 210 yd (192 m); C: 180 yd (165 m); D: 175 yd (160 m); E: 197 yd (180 m)

SPECIAL STITCH:

dc2tog: On Round 8 only, leaving sts unfinished, dc in same ch-5 sp, skip sc, dc in next ch-5 sp, yo and draw through all loops on hook. On all other rounds, leaving sts unfinished, dc in next st, skip 1 st, dc in next st, yo and draw through all loops on hook.

thb: Work through the horizontal bar at the back of each st and through all 3 horizontal bars on decrease sts.

Method

FOUNDATION RING:

With Color A, make a Magic Ring.

ROUND 1: Ch 5 (counts as 1 dc, ch 2), [dc into the ring, ch 2] 5 times, join with sl st in 3rd ch of beg-ch.

ROUND 2: Sl st into next ch-sp, [(ch 3, 3 dc, ch 3, sl st) in ch-sp, sl st in next dc] 6 times, end Color A.

ROUND 3: Join Color B in sl st between two petals, ch 7 (counts as 1 dc, ch 4), [dc in next sl st between petals, ch 4] 5 times, join with sl st in 3rd ch of beg-ch.

ROUND 4: Sl st into next ch-sp, [(ch 3, 4 dc, ch 3, sl st) in ch-sp, sl st in next dc] 6 times, end Color B.

ROUND 5: Join Color C in sl st between petals, ch 8 (counts as 1 dc, ch 5), [dc in next sl st between petals, ch 5] 5 times, join with sl st in 3rd ch of beg-ch.

ROUND 6: Sl st into next ch-sp, [(ch 3, 5 dc, ch 3, sl st) in ch-sp, sl st in next dc] 6 times, end Color C.

ROUND 7: Join Color D thb of 3rd dc of petal, ch 1 and sc in same place, * ch 5, BPsc around dc of Round 3, ch 5 **, sc thb of 3rd dc of next petal; rep from * 4 more times, rep from * to ** once, join with sl st in first sc.

ROUND 8: Ch 3 (counts as 1 dc), (dc, ch 2, 2 dc) in same place, * 4 dc in ch-5 sp, dc2tog, 4 dc in next ch-5 sp **, (2 dc, ch 2, 2 dc) in next st; rep from * 4 more times, rep from * to ** once, join with sl st in first st, end Color D.

ROUND 9: Join Color B in ch-2 sp, ch 3 (counts as 1 dc), (dc, ch 2, 2 dc) in same place, * dc in each st to 1 st before dec, dc2tog, dc in each st to ch-sp **, (2 dc, ch 2, 2 dc) in ch-sp; rep from * 4 more times, rep from * to ** once, join with sl st in first st, end Color B.

ROUND 10: Rep Round 9 using Color A.

ROUND 11: Rep Round 9 using Color E.

ROUND 12: Rep Round 9 using Color C.

ROUND 13: Rep Round 9 using Color E.

ROUND 14: Rep Round 9 using Color A.

ROUND 15: Rep Round 9 using Color B.

ROUND 16: Rep Round 9 using Color D.

Rep Rounds 9–16 for pattern until 25 rounds have been worked.

ch
sl st
sc
sc thb
dc
BPsc
dc2tog
magic ring
beginning of round

Candy Rose

A
B
C
D

Follow instructions using alternative colors.

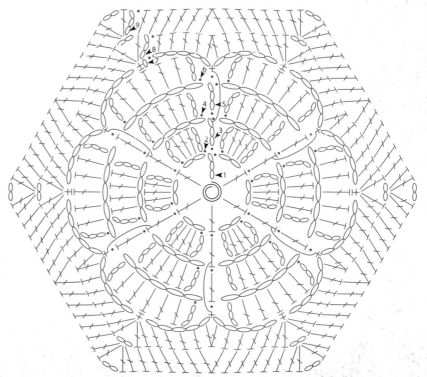

Buttons

- **SKILL LEVEL:** Advanced
- **MEASUREMENT:** One pattern repeat = 6¼ in. (16 cm) wide x 3½ in. (9 cm) high

SPECIAL STITCH:

dc2tog: Leaving sts unfinished, dc in next st, skip 1 st, dc in next st, yo and draw through all loops on hook.

dc3tog: Leaving sts unfinished, dc in next 3 sts or ch, yo and draw through all loops on hook.

- A
- B
- C
- D
- E

Method

CIRCLES:
Make one each in Color A, B, and C for each multiple, plus 1 in Color A.
FOUNDATION RING: Make a Magic Ring.
ROUND 1: Ch 3 (counts as 1 dc), 15 dc into ring, join with sl st in 3rd of beginning ch-3, end color.

RIPPLE:

ROW 1: With Color D, join with sl st in any st of circle in Color A, ch 3, dc in next st, * dc in each of next 2 sts of circle, 3 dc in next st, dc in each of next 2 sts of circle **, dc2tog in next st of Circle 1 and st of Circle 2; rep from * until 1 circle remains, rep from * to **, dc2tog in last 2 sts, turn.
ROW 2: Ch 3, dc in next st, *dc in each of next 2 sts, 3 dc in next st **, dc in each of next 2 sts, dc3tog; rep from * until 7 sts remain, rep from * to **, dc in each of next 2 sts, dc2tog in last 2 sts, end Color D, turn.
ROW 3: Join Color E, ch 3, dc in next st, dc in each of next 2 sts, 3 dc in next st, dc in each of next 2 sts, * dc3tog, dc in each of next 2 sts, 3 dc in next st, dc in each of next 2 sts, rep from * until 2 sts remain, dc2tog in last 2 sts, turn.
ROW 4: Rep Row 2, end Color E.
ROW 5: Join Color D to last row and rep Row 1 working into sts of the last row at the same time. Rep Rows 2–5 for pattern.

Manhattan

Follow instructions using alternative colors:

ROWS 1–4: Color D
ROW 5: Color E
ROWS 6–8: Rep Rows 2–4 using Color E
ROW 9: Rep Row 5 using Color F
ROW 10–12: Rep Row 2 using Color F
Rep Rows 1–12 for pattern.

▧	A
■	B
□	C
▨	D
▥	E
▦	F

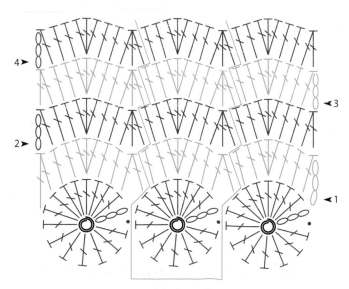

Multiple of 7 + 16 ch

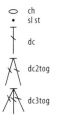

⬭ ch
• sl st
┼ dc
⋀ dc2tog
⋔ dc3tog
◄ beginning of row/round

Sea Foam

- **SKILL LEVEL:** Advanced
- **MEASUREMENT:** One pattern repeat =
  6¼ in. (16 cm) wide x 3½ in. (9 cm) high

■ A
■ B
■ C
■ D
□ E

SPECIAL STITCH:

sc2tog: Leaving sts unfinished, sc in next 2 sts, yo and draw through all loops on hook.

dc2tog: On Row 1 only, leaving sts unfinished, dc in next 2 ch, yo and draw through all loops on hook. On all other rows, leaving sts unfinished, dc in next 2 sts, yo and draw through all loops on hook.

Method

FOUNDATION CHAIN: With Color A, ch a multiple of 22 ch, turn foundation ch.

ROW 1: Ch 3 (counts as 1 dc), dc in 4th ch from hook, * dc in next 8 ch, [dc2tog] twice, dc in next 8 ch **, [2 dc in next ch] twice; rep from * until 21 ch remain, rep from * to ** once, 2 dc in last ch, end Color A, turn.

ROW 2: Join Color B, ch 3 (counts as 1 dc), dc in same place, dc in next 8 sts, [dc2tog] twice, dc in next 8 sts, * [2 dc in next st] twice, dc in next 8 sts, [dc2tog] twice, dc in next 8 sts; rep from * until 1 st remains, 2 dc in last st, end Color B, turn.

ROW 3: Join Color C, ch 3 (counts as 1 dc), dc in same place, * dc in next 8 sts, [dc2tog] twice, dc in next 8 sts **, [2 dc in next st] twice; rep from * until 21 sts remain, rep from * to ** once, 2 dc in last st, end Color C, turn.

ROW 4: Join Color D, ch 1, 2 sc in same place, sc in next 8 sts, [sc2tog] twice, sc in next 8 sts, * [2 sc in next st] twice, sc in next 8 sts, [sc2tog] twice, sc in next 8 sts; rep from * until 1 st remains, 2 sc in last st, end Color D, turn.

ROW 5: Join Color E through front loop only, ch 4, sl st tfl of next st; rep from * to end, end Color E, turn.

ROW 6: Join Color D tfl only, ch 1, 2 sc tfl in same place, sc tfl in next 8 sts, [sc2tog tfl] twice, sc tfl in next 8 sts, * [2 sc tfl in next st] twice, sc tfl in next 8 sts, [sc2tog tfl] twice, sc tfl in next 8 sts; rep from * until 1 st remains, 2 sc tfl in last st, end Color D, turn.

ROW 7: Join Color A, ch 3 (counts as 1 dc), dc in same place, * dc in next 8 sts, [dc2tog] twice, dc in next 8 sts **, [2 dc in next st] twice; rep from * until 21 sts remain, rep from * to ** once, 2 dc in last st, end Color A, turn.

Rep Rows 2–7 for pattern.

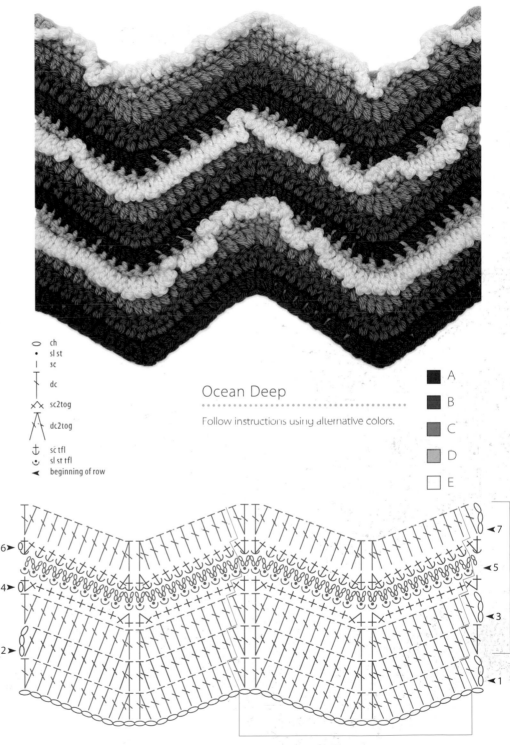

⬯	ch
•	sl st
		sc
⊺	dc
⤬	sc2tog
⨉	dc2tog
⚓	sc tfl
☺	sl st tfl
◄	beginning of row

Ocean Deep

Follow instructions using alternative colors.

■ A
■ B
■ C
■ D
□ E

Multiple of 22 ch

Mountain Streams

A
B
C
D

- **SKILL LEVEL:** Advanced
- **MEASUREMENT:** One pattern repeat = 2 in. (5 cm) wide x 4 in. (10 cm) high

SPECIAL STITCH:

Beg scdec: At the start of a row, leaving sts unfinished, sc in next 2 sts, yo and draw through all loops on hook.

End scdec: At the end of a row, leaving sts unfinished, sc in last 2 sts of the row, yo and draw through all loops on hook.

sc2tog: Leaving sts unfinished, sc in next st, skip 1 st, sc in next st, yo and draw through all loops on hook.

dc2tog: Leaving sts unfinished, dc in next 2 sts, yo and draw through all loops on hook.

dc3tog: Leaving sts unfinished, dc in next 3 sts, yo and draw through all loops on hook.

thb: Work through the horizontal bar at the back of each st.

Method

FOUNDATION CHAIN: With Color A, ch a multiple of 6 + 1, turn foundation chain.

ROW 1: Ch 1, sc in 2nd ch from hook, hdc in next ch, dc in next ch, 3 dc in next ch, * dc in next ch, hdc in next ch, sc in next ch, hdc in next ch, dc in next ch, 3 dc in next ch; rep from * to last 3 ch, dc in next ch, hdc in next ch, sc in last ch, end Color A, turn.

ROW 2: Join Color B thb, ch 1, beg scdec thb, sc thb in each of next 2 sts, * 3 sc thb in next st, sc thb in each of next 2 sts, sc2tog thb, sc thb in each of next 2 sts; rep from * to last 5 sts, 3 sc thb in next st, sc thb in each of next 2 sts, end scdec thb in last 2 sts, turn.

ROW 3: Ch 1, beg scdec, sc in each of next 2 sts, 3 sc in next st, * sc in each of next 2 sts, sc2tog, sc in each of next 2 sts, 3 sc in next st; rep from * to last 4 sts, sc in each of next 2 sts, end scdec in last 2 sts, end Color B, turn.

ROW 4: Join Color C, ch 1, Beg scdec, sc in each of next 2 sts, * 3 sc in next st, sc in each of next 2 sts, sc2tog, sc in each of next 2 sts; rep from * to last 5 sts, 3 sc in next st, sc in each of next 2 sts, end scdec in last 2 sts, turn.

ROW 5: Repeat Row 3, end Color C, turn.

ROW 6: Join Color D, ch 2, dc thb in next st (decrease made), dc thb in next st, hdc thb in next st, * sc thb in next st, hdc thb in next st, dc thb in next st, dc3tog thb in next st, dc thb in next st, hdc thb in next st; rep from * to last 5 sts, sc thb in next st, hdc thb in next st, dc thb in next st, dc2tog thb in next st, turn.

ROW 7: Ch 3 (counts as 1 dc), dc in same place, dc in next st, hdc in next st, sc in next st, * hdc in next st, dc in next st, 3 dc in next st, dc in next st, hdc in next st, sc in next st; rep from * to last 3 sts, hdc in next st, dc in next st, 2 dc in last st, end Color D, turn.

ROW 8: Join Color C, ch 1, 2 sc in same place, sc thb in each of next 2 sts, * sc2tog thb, sc thb in each of next 2 sts, 3 sc thb in next st, sc thb in each of next 2 sts; rep from * to last 6 sts, sc2tog thb, sc thb in each of next 2 sts, 2 sc thb in last st, turn.

ROW 9: Ch 1, 2 sc in same place, sc in each of next 2 sts, sc2tog, * sc in each of next 2 sts, 3 sc in next st, sc in each of next 2 sts, sc2tog; rep from * to last 3 sts, sc in each of next 2 sts, 2 sc in last st, end Color C, turn.

ROW 10: Join Color B, ch 1, 2 sc in same place, sc in each of next 2 sts, * sc2tog, sc in each of next 2 sts, 3 sc in next st, sc in each of next 2 sts; rep from * to last 5 sts, sc2tog, sc in each of next 2 sts, 2 sc in last st, turn.

ROW 11: Repeat Row 9, end Color B, turn.

ROW 12: Join Color A thb, ch 1, sc thb in same place, hdc thb in next st, dc thb in next st, * dc3tog thb, dc thb in next st, hdc thb in next st, sc thb in next st, hdc thb in next st, dc thb in next st; rep from * to last 6 sts, dc3tog thb, dc thb in next st, hdc thb in next st, sc thb in last st, turn.

ROW 13: Ch 1, sc in same place, hdc in next st, dc in next st, 3 dc in next st, * dc in next st, hdc in next st, sc in next st, hdc in next st, dc in next st, 3 dc in next st; rep from * to last 3 sts, dc in next st, hdc in next st, sc in last st, end Color A, turn.

Repeat Rows 2–13 for pattern.

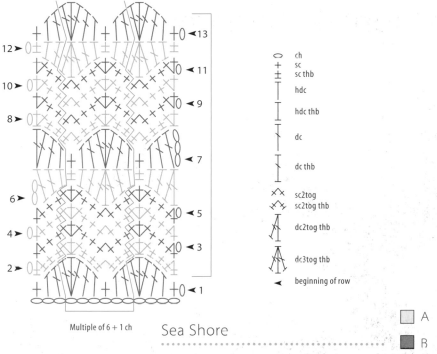

Multiple of 6 + 1 ch

⊖	ch
+	sc
‡	sc thb
⊥	hdc
	hdc thb
	dc
	dc thb
✕✕	sc2tog
	sc2tog thb
	dc2tog thb
	dc3tog thb
◄	beginning of row

Sea Shore

Follow instructions using alternative colors.

ROW 1: Color A

ROWS 2–5: Color B

ROWS 6–7: Color A

ROWS 8–11: Color B

ROWS 12–13: Color A

Repeat Rows 2–13 for pattern.

□ A

■ B

Candy Floss

A
B
C
D

....

- **SKILL LEVEL:** Advanced
- **MEASUREMENT:** One pattern repeat =
  4¼ in. (11 cm) wide x 5 in. (13 cm) high

SPECIAL STITCH:

dc-dec: On Row 1 only, leaving sts unfinished,
dc in next ch, skip 3 ch, dc in next ch, yo and
draw through all loops on hook.
On Rows 2–4 only, leaving sts unfinished, dc
in next ch, skip 1 st, dc in next ch, yo and draw
through all loops on hook.
On Rows 5–7 only, leaving sts unfinished, dc
in next st, skip 1 st, dc in next st, yo and draw
through all loops on hook.

Method

FOUNDATION CHAIN: With Color A, ch a multiple
of 20 + 1, turn foundation chain.

ROW 1: Ch 3 (counts as 1 dc), 1 dc in 4th ch from
hook, * [ch 1, skip 1 ch, dc in next ch] 3 times,
ch 1, skip 1 ch, dc-dec, [ch 1, skip 1 ch, dc in next
ch] 3 times, ch 1, skip 1 ch **, (dc, ch 2, dc) in next
ch; rep from * to last 20 ch, rep from * to ** once,
2 dc in last ch, turn.

ROW 2: Ch 3 (counts as 1 dc), dc in same place,
[ch 1, skip 1, dc in ch-sp] 3 times, ch 1, skip 1 st,
dc-dec, [ch 1, skip 1 st, dc in ch-sp] 3 times, ch 1,
skip 1 st, * (dc, ch 2, dc) in ch-2 sp, [ch 1, skip 1 st,
dc in ch-sp] 3 times, ch 1, skip 1 st, dc-dec, [ch 1,
skip 1 st, dc in ch-sp] 3 times, ch 1, skip 1 st; rep
from * to last st, 2 dc in last st, turn.

ROW 3: Ch 3 (counts as 1 dc), dc in same place,
* [ch 1, skip 1 st, dc in ch-sp] 3 times, ch 1, skip
1 st, dc-dec, [ch 1, skip 1 st, dc in ch-sp] 3 times,
ch 1, skip 1 st **, (dc, ch 2, dc) in ch-2 sp; rep
from * to last 10 sts, rep from * to ** once,
2 dc in last st, turn.

ROW 4: Ch 3 (counts as 1 dc), dc in same place,
dc in each of next 7 sts and ch-sp, dc-dec, dc
in each of next 7 sts and ch-sp, * (dc, ch 2, dc)
in ch-2 sp, dc in each of next 7 sts and ch-sp,
dc-dec, dc in each of next 7 sts and ch-sp; rep
from * to last st, 2 dc in last st, turn.

ROW 5: Ch 3 (counts as 1 dc), dc in same place, *
dc in each of next 7 sts, dc-dec, dc in each of next
7 sts **, (dc, ch 2, dc) in ch-2 sp; rep from * to last
18 sts, rep from * to ** once, 2 dc in last st, turn.

ROW 6: Ch 3 (counts as 1 dc), dc in same place, dc
in each of next 7 sts, dc-dec, dc in each of next

7 sts, * (dc, ch 2, dc) in ch-2 sp, dc in each of next 7 sts, dc-dec, dc in each of next 7 sts; rep from * to last st, 2 dc in last st, turn.

ROW 7: Ch 3 (counts as 1 dc), dc in same place, * [ch 1, skip 1 st, dc in next st] 3 times, ch 1, dc-dec, [ch 1, skip 1 st, dc in next st] 3 times, ch 1, skip 1 st **, (dc, ch 2, dc) in ch-2 sp; rep from * to last 18 sts, rep from * to ** once, 2 dc in last st, turn. Repeat Rows 2–7 for pattern.

SURFACE CROCHET:

Join Color B around post of second st on Row 1, ch 3 (counts as 1 dc), 3 dc around post working from bottom of stitch to top, * ch 1, 4 dc around post of next st working from top of stitch to bottom, ch 1, 4 dc around post of next st working from bottom of stitch to top, rep from * across to 2nd to last stitch, work 3 dc around post of stitch, ch 3, sl st around post, end Color B. Repeat on Row 7, then every 7th row throughout. Repeat instructions on Row 2, using Color C, then every 7th row throughout. Repeat instructions on Row 3, using Color D, then every 7th row throughout.

Ruffle Ripple

Follow instructions using alternative colors.

⬜	A
⬛	B
⬛	C
⬜	D

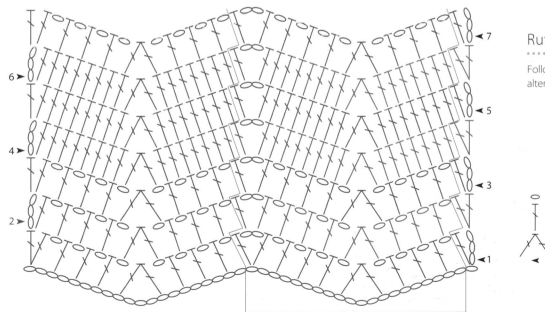

Multiple of 20 + 1 ch

Sea of Hearts

- **SKILL LEVEL:** Advanced
- **MEASUREMENT:** One pattern repeat =
  4¼ in. (11 cm) wide x 4 in. (10 cm) high

SPECIAL STITCH:

dc3tog: Leaving sts unfinished, dc in next
3 sts, yo and draw through all loops on hook.

A
B
C
D

Method

FOUNDATION CHAIN: With Color A, ch a multiple of 14 + 1, turn foundation chain.

ROW 1 (RS): Ch 3 (counts as 1 dc), dc into 4th ch from hook, * dc in each of next 5 ch, dc3tog over next 3 ch, dc in each of next 5 ch, (dc, ch 1, dc) in next ch; rep from * to last 14 ch, dc in each of next 5 ch, dc3tog over next 3 ch, dc in each of next 5 ch, 2 dc in last ch, end Color A, turn.

ROW 2 (WS): Join Color B, ch 3 (counts as 1 dc), dc in same place, dc in each of next 5 sts, dc3tog over next 3 sts, dc in each of next 5 sts, * 3 dc in ch-1 sp, dc in each of next 5 sts, dc3tog over next 3 sts, dc in each of next 5 sts; rep from * to last st, 2 dc in last st, end Color B, turn.

ROW 3: Join Color C, ch 3 (counts as 1 dc), dc in same place, * dc in each of next 5 sts, dc3tog over next 3 sts, dc in each of next 5 sts, 3 dc in next st; rep from * to last 14 sts, dc in each of next 5 sts, dc3tog over next 3 sts, dc in each of next 5 sts, 2 dc in last st, end Color C, turn.

ROW 4: Repeat Row 2 using Color B.

ROW 5: Join Color A, ch 3 (counts as 1 dc) and dc in same place, * dc in each of next 5 sts, dc3tog over next 3 sts, dc in each of next 5 sts, (dc, ch 1, dc) in next st; rep from * to last 14 sts, dc in each of next 5 st, dc3tog over next 3 sts, dc in each of next 5 sts, 2 dc in last st, end Color A, turn.

Repeat Rows 2–5. Work hearts after each pattern repeat.

SURFACE CROCHET HEARTS:

Each heart is worked over the posts of (dc, ch 1, dc) on Row 1, then every repeat of Row 5.

ROUND 1: With RS facing, join Color D by working a sl st around the post at bottom of first dc of (dc, ch 1, dc), ch 1, (sc, hdc, 3 dc) around post, ch 2, sl st around top of same post, ch 1, sl st around top of post of 2nd dc of (dc, ch 1, dc), ch 2, (3 dc, hdc, sc) around post, ch 2, join with sl st in top of beginning-ch.

ROUND 2: Ch 1 and sc in same place, sc in each of next 3 sts, 2 sc in next st, 2 sc in first ch of ch-2, sc in next ch, sl st in ch-1 sp, sc in first ch of ch-2, 2 sc in next ch, 2 sc in next st, sc in each of next 4 sts, (sc, ch 2, sc) in ch-sp, join with sl st in top of beginning-ch. End Color D. Weave in ends.

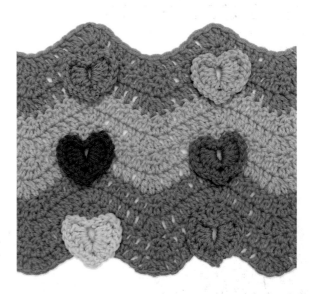

Valentine's Day

Use scraps of yarn for the hearts.

Follow instructions above using alternative colors:

ROWS 1–4: Color A
ROWS 5–8: Color B
Repeat Rows 1–8, changing colors every 4 rows.

A
B

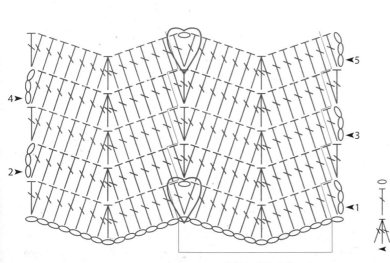

	ch
	dc
	dc3tog
◄	beginning of row/round

Multiple of 14 + 1 ch

○	ch
•	sl st
+	sc
	hdc
	dc
◄	beginning of row/round

PROJECT
Scarf: Botticelli

A

B

C

D

E

F

G

- **SKILL LEVEL:** Advanced
- **MEASUREMENT:** Finished size = 69 in. (175 cm) x 11 in. (28 cm)
- **HOOK SIZE:** H-8 (5 mm)
- **YARN WEIGHT:** DK
- **YARN AMOUNT:** A: 84 yd (77 m); B: 49 yd (45 m); C: 49 yd (45 m); D: 49 yd (45 m); E: 49 yd (45 m); F: 49 yd (45 m); G: 49 yd (45 m)

SPECIAL STITCH:

sc3tog: Leaving sts unfinished, sc in next 3 sts, yo and draw through all loops on hook.

dc3tog: On Row 1, leaving sts unfinished, dc in next 3 ch, yo and draw through all loops on hook.

On all other rows, leaving sts unfinished, dc in next 3 sts, yo and draw through all loops on hook.

thb: Work through the horizontal bar at the back of each st and through all 3 horizontal bars on decrease sts.

Method

FOUNDATION CHAIN: With Color A, ch 241 (or a multiple of 8 + 9), turn foundation chain.

ROW 1: Ch 3 (counts as 1 dc), dc in 4th ch from hook, * dc in each of next 2 ch, dc3tog, dc in each of next 2 ch **, 3 dc in next ch; rep from * until 8 ch remain, rep from * to ** once, 2 dc in last ch, end Color A, do not turn.

ROW 2: Join Color B thb, ch 1, 2 sc thb in same place, * sc thb in each of next 2 sts, sc3tog thb, sc thb in each of next 2 sts **, 3 sc thb in next st; rep from * until 8 sts remain, rep from * to ** once, 2 sc thb in last st, end Color B, do not turn.

ROW 3: Join Color C thb, ch 3 (counts as 1 dc), dc in same place, * dc thb in each of next 2 sts, dc3tog thb, dc thb in each of next 2 sts **, 3 dc thb in next st; rep from * until 8 sts remain, rep from * to ** once, 2 dc thb in last st, end Color C, do not turn.

ROWS 4–15: Rep Rows 2–3 for pattern, changing color on each row, ending with Color A. Fasten off.

EDGES:

At each end of the scarf, join Color A in a corner, ch 1 and work 1 row of sc, working 2 sc around each dc and 1 sc around each sc across, end Color A.
Fasten off. Weave in ends

Glacier

Follow instructions using alternative colors.

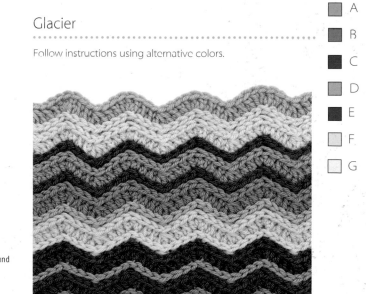

A

B

C

D

E

F

G

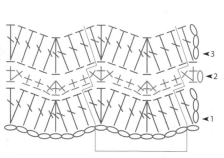

Multiple of 8 + 9 ch

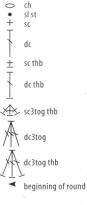

◁ 3

◁ 2

◁ 1

○   ch
●   sl st
+   sc
╪   dc
±   sc thb
╪   dc thb
⩞   sc3tog thb
⋀   dc3tog
⋀   dc3tog thb
◁   beginning of round

Index

A

abbreviations 18
afghans
  Candy Rose 113
  Coral Reef 45
  Ice Cream Sundae 44–45
  Retro Rose 112–113
acrylic 8
Amethyst 67
appliqué motifs 21
Arcade 48–49
Aspen 90–91

B

back post double crochet
  (BPdc) 14
bags
  Amalfi 87
  Charleston 86–87
bead stitch 15
beads 21
Berry Ripple 66–67
Big Dipper 105
Bloomsbury Bobble 85
Blue Ridge 103
bobble (B) 12
Bobbled Zig-zag 84–85
Bonfire 101
Bright Burst 50–51
Bright Waves 26–27
Butterfly 30–31
Buttons 114–115
buttons 21

C

Candy Floss 120–121
chains
  foundation chains 10–11
  turning and starting chains 11
charts 18–19
  charts in rounds 19
  charts in rows 19
cluster (Cl) 14
colors, changing 17
  joining 17
combination yarns 8

Compact Chevrons 42–43
Confetti 96–97
Contrast Ripple 43
cotton 8
cotton mixes 8
crochet hooks 9
  holding the hook and yarn 10

D

decreases 15
double crochet (dc) 12
  turning chains 11
double treble crochet (dtr) 11
  turning chains 11

E

Easter 109
edgings 20
  working across top or bottom
    edge 20
  working along sides of row
    ends 20
  working around corners 20
embellishments 21
embroidery 21
ends, weaving in 17
equipment 8–9

F

Fall Leaves 54–55
Ferris Wheel 110–111
Flames 32–33
Floral Pop 51
Florence 39
Flower Meadow 97
Forest Star 47
foundation chains 10
  turning foundation chain 11
Foundation Ring 16
front post double crochet
  (FPdc) 14
Fuchsia Flower 70–71

G

gauge 19

H

half double crochet (hdc) 12
  turning chains 11
Halloween 73
Harmony 31
Harvest 100–101
Hill and Valley 28–29
holding the hook and yarn 10
Honeydew 56–57
Hot Star 46–47

I

Indigo Vs 41

J

Jasmine 52–53

K

Kaleidoscope 98–99
Kyoto 95

L

Lavender Layers 68–69

M

Magic Ring 16
Manhattan 115
Marrakesh 49
materials 8
measuring tapes 9
Merlot 63
Metro 79
Mille-Feuille 34–35
Moss Bank 55
Mountain Streams 118–119
Mulberry Whip 93

N

Natural Granny 25
Neapolitan 57
needles 9
notions 9
novelty yarns 8

O

Ocean Deep 117
Ocean Swell 102–103
Orion's Belt 104–105

P

Parisian Bobble 77
Pastel Posy 70–71
patterns 18–19
Periwinkle 53
pillows
  Glade 65
  San Francisco 64–65
Pink Denim 58–59
Pink Haze 92–93
pins 9
Plum Strata 91
popcorn (PC) 15
posts, working round 14
projects
  afghan—Candy Rose 113
  afghan—Coral Reef 45
  afghan—Ice Cream
    Sundae 44–45
  afghan—Retro Rose 112–113
  bag—Amalfi 87
  bag—Charleston 86–87
  pillow—Glade 65
  pillow—San Francisco
    64–65
  purse—Jitterbug 88–89
  scarf—Botticelli 124–125
  scarf—Glacier 125
puff stitch (PS) 14
Pumpkin Patch 72–73
Purple Picots 74–75
purse
  Jitterbug 88–89
Pyrotechnics 33

R

Rainbow Granny 24–25
Rainbow Road 36–37
Raspberry Ripple 107
reading patterns and charts
  18–19

Red, Stripe and Blue 76–77
Rhythm 60–61
ribbons 21
Rock Pool 78–79
Roman Blinds 80–81
Rosette 111
rounds 16
  charts 19
  finishing off final round 16
  Foundation Ring 16
  Magic Ring 16
  working into the ring 16
rows
  changing colors at the start or
    middle of a row 17
  charts in rows 19
Ruffle Ripple 121
rulers 9

S

scarves
  Botticelli 124–125
  Glacier 125
scissors 9
Sea Foam 116–117
Sea of Hearts 122–123
Sea Shore 119
Seventies Groove 61
Shamrock Ripple 75
Shell Ripple 82–83
Shinto 94–95
Shock Wave 81
single crochet (sc) 11
  turning chain 11
slip knots 10
slip stitch (sl st) 11
Sorbet 69
spike stitch (Ss) 15
Springtime 99
starting chains 11
stitch markers 9
stitches 10
  back post double crochet
    (BPdc) 13
  bead stitch 15
  bobble (B) 14

cluster (Cl) 14
decreases 15
double crochet (dc) 12
double treble crochet
    (dtr) 11
front post double crochet
    (FPdc) 13
half double crochet (hdc) 12
popcorn (PC) 15
puff stitch (PS) 14
single crochet (sc) 11
slip stitch 11
spike stitch (Ss) 15
treble crochet (tr) 12–13
Strawberry Mint 106–107
Summer Ripple 83
surface crochet 17, 21
    charts 19
symbols 18
    arrangements of symbols 18
Syrah 62–63

T
techniques
    changing colors at the start or
        middle of a row 17
    finishing off final round 16
    foundation chain 10
    holding the hook and yarn 10
    joining a new color when
        working in the round 17
    making a Foundation Ring 16
    making a Magic Ring 16
    making a slip knot 10
    surface crochet 17
    turning and starting
        chains 11
    turning foundation chain 11
    weaving in ends 17
    working in rounds 16
    working into the ring 16
Tiramisu 35
Topography 29
treble crochet (tr) 12–13
    turning chains 11
Tulips 108–109

turning chains 11
Tuscan Horizon 37

V
Valentine's Day 123
Venice 38–39
Vibrant Vs 40–41
Vibrate 59

W
weaving in ends 17
wool 8
working round posts 14

Y
yarns 8
    calculating yarn amounts 19
    holding the hook and
        yarn 10
    yarn labels 9

Credits

Thank you to everyone at Quarto who has worked on the book—have another dip in the cookie jar for a job well done! Thank you to Kang for turning my scribbles into legible charts and to Therese for turning my patterns into legible text. Last but not least, thanks to Veronica and Sean… I promise not to talk about ripples for a while.

References:
75 Floral Blocks to Crochet Betty Barnden
200 Crochet Blocks Jan Eaton
Easy Crocheted Accessories Carol Meldrum

All other photographs and illustrations are the copyright of Quarto Publishing plc. While every effort has been made to credit contributors, Quarto would like to apologize should there have been any omissions or errors—and would be pleased to make the appropriate correction for future editions of the book.

With special thanks to Cascade Yarns for providing the yarns used in this book. All yarns are from the Cascade 220 range and are detailed on page 128.
www.cascadeyarns.com

Cascade Yarns List

Every effort has been made to list the correct color number from the Cascade 220 range of yarns, but please use the following list as a guide only and be sure to check exact colors with your yarn supplier before purchasing.

KEY
Page number/name of square/color code in book/
Cascade 220 range (where relevant)/Cascade color number

pp. 24–25 Rainbow Granny
A 901, B 821, C 886, D 810, E 1973, F 842; **Natural Granny** A 1973, B 886, C 821

pp. 26–27 Bright Waves A 887, B 847, C 842, D 901, E 1952; **Atlantic Waves** A 906, B 887, C 848, D 847, E 1986, F 842

pp. 28–29 Hill and Valley A 803, B 811, C 1985, D 850, E 1915; **Topography** A 1985, B 850, C 1915, D 836, E 1967

pp. 30–31 Butterfly A 840, B 836, C 1942; **Harmony** A 897, B 840, C 850

pp. 32–33 Flames A 808, B 907, C 825, D 877, E 820, F 910A; **Pyrotechnics** A 808, B 825, C 820, D 901, E 842, F 1986

pp. 34–35 Mille-Feuille A 1973, B 1942, C 817, D 1941, E 827, F 873, G 875; **Tiramisu** A 873, B 827, C 817, D 1973

pp. 36–37 Rainbow Road A 808, B 839, C 820, D 887, E 810, F 849, G 883; **Tuscan Horizon** A 887, B 810, C 849, D 883, E 1967

pp. 38–39 Venice A 914A, B 1942, C 834, D 817, E 842, F 1973; **Florence** A 884, B 834, C 897, D 824, E 1940, F 1942

pp. 40–41 Vibrant Vs A 887, B 883, C 822, D 837, E 879; **Indigo Vs** A 837, B 879, C 885, D 883, E 884

pp. 42–43 Compact Chevrons A 819, B 822, C 886, D 910A, E 849;

Contrast Ripple A 802, B 907, C 850, D 823

pp. 44–45 Ice-cream Sundae A 8902, B 7812, C 8908, D 7809, E 8912, F 7803, G 9469, H 9477, I 8021; **Coral Reef** A 837, B 908, C 875, D 903, E 836

pp. 46–47 Hot Star A 820, B 825, C 907, D 1922; **Forest Star** A 1915, B 850, C 841, D 801

pp. 48–49 Arcade A 820, B 892, C 816, D 877; **Marrakesh** A 886, B 877, C 816

pp. 50–51 Bright Burst A 851, B 809, C 907, D 810; **Floral Pop** A 810, B 851, C 807, D 1986

pp. 52–53 Jasmine A 816, B 837, C 875; **Periwinkle** A 875, B 914A, C 804

pp. 54–55 Fall Leaves A 811, B 841, C 907, D 821; **Moss Bank** A 821, B 886, C 841, D 801

pp. 56–57 Honeydew A 827, B 850, C 1915; **Neapolitan** A 827, B 873, C 1915

pp. 58–59 Pink Denim A 904, B 834, C 910A, D 837; **Vibrate** A 1944, B 834, C 1941, D 837

pp. 60–61 Rhythm A 1971, B 822, C 821, D 820, E 850, F 810, G 811; **book cover** A 8908, B 8912, C 9541, D 9478, E 9469, F 7828, G 7827, H 4147, I 8910, J 7812, K 8891, L 8906; **70s Groove** A 811, B 822, C 810, D 850, E 821

pp. 62–63 Syrah A 842, B 857,

C 880, D 893, E 809, F 837; **Merlot** A 837, B 809, C 893

pp. 64–65 San Francisco 12 in. (30 cm) Pillow A 8509, B 7815, C 9541, D 8912, E 9477, F 8913, G 9469, H 9422; **18 in. (45 cm) Pillow** A 8895, B 9422, C 9477, D 9469, E 9541, F 8912, G 7815, H 8509; **20 in. (50 cm) Pillow** A 8010, B 9422, C 9541, D 8912, E 7815, F 9477, G 8895; **Glade** A 1793, B 812, C 810, D 1960, E 802, F 887, G 851

pp. 66–67 Berry Ripple A 1967, B 851, C 837; **Amethyst** A 892, B 1967, C 837

pp. 68–69 Lavender Layers A 1971, B 834, C 844, D 1915, E 1914, F 910A; **Sorbet** A 834, B 1915, C 910A

pp. 70–71 Pastel Posy A 871, B 850, C 894, D 897, E 808; **Fuschia Flower** A 850, B 836, C 901, D 903, E 809

pp. 72–73 Pumpkin Patch A 801, B 802, C 1952, D 820; **Halloween** A 825, B 851, C 802, D 910A

pp. 74–75 Purple Picots A 807, B 871, C 851, D 1967; **Shamrock Ripple** A 881, B 875, C 851, D 891

pp. 76–77 Red, Stripe, and Blue A 883, B 885, C 871, D 1922, E 808; **Parisian Bobble** A 808, B 871, C 883

pp. 78–79 Rock Pool A 883, B 884, C 887, D 1922, E 877; **Metro** A 904, B 1944, C 907, D 817, E 887

pp. 80–81 Roman Blinds A 804, B 1985, C 850, D 840; **Shock Wave** A 903, B 807, C 804, D 840

pp. 82–83 Shell Ripple A 824, B 901, C 847, D 851; **Summer Ripple** A 824, B 871, C 851, D 901, E 808

pp. 84–85 Bobbled Zig-zag A 875, B 823, C 818; **Bloomsbury Bobble** A 1944, B 1914, C 873

pp. 86–89 Charleston A 815, B 879, C 851, D 1985, E 892, F 811, G 886, H 890, I 816, J 810; **Amalfi** A 811, B 887, C 810; **Jitterbug** A 815, B 886, C 879, D 892, E 811, F 810

pp. 90–91 Aspen A 903, B 835, C 873, D 875, E 1942; **Plum Strata** A 816, B 875, C 879, D 903

pp. 92–93 Pink Haze A 908, B 914A, C 836, D 894; **Mulberry Whip** A 882, B 857, C 842

pp. 94–95 Shinto A 816, B 850, C 840; **Kyoto** A 1986, B 906, C 804, D 842

pp. 96–97 Confetti A 906, B 903, C 842, D 825, E 820; **Flower Meadow** A 906, B 809, C 820

pp. 98–99 Kaleidoscope A 820, B 1952, C 851, C 897, E 901; **Springtime** A 897, B 851, C 820

pp. 100–101 Harvest A 823, B 872, C 822, D 1922; **Bonfire** A 1961, B 817, C 1922, D 822

pp. 102–103 Ocean Swell A 851, B 1973, C 811; **Blue Ridge** A 824, B 851, C 812

pp. 104–105 Orion's Belt A 824, B 883, C 914A, D 847; **Big Dipper** A 836, B 824, C 908, D 914A

pp. 106–107 Strawberry Mint A 850, B 839, C 809; **Raspberry Ripple**, A 839, B 809, C 893

pp. 108–109 Tulips A 837, B 802, C 824; **Easter** A 824, B 825, C 1973

pp. 110–111 Ferris Wheel A 850, B 1967, C 914A; **Rosette** A 850, B 840, C 894

pp. 112–113 Retro Rose A 9605, B 7827, C 7812, D 8505, E 8908; **Candy Rose** A 8505, B 7805, C 9422, D 8908

pp. 114–115 Buttons A 1973, B 892, C 850, D 816, E 827; **Manhattan** A 892, B 816, C 871, D 907, E 851, F 812

pp. 116–117 Sea Foam A 890,

B 849, C 1973, D 821, E 817; **Ocean Deep** A 885, B 883, C 884, D 1973, E 871

pp. 118–119 Mountain Streams A 877, B 813, C 841, D 821; **Sea Shore** A 821, B 814

pp. 120–121 Candy Floss A 875, B 827, C 1940, D 1941; **Ruffle Ripple** A 835, B 837, C 839, D 874

pp. 122–123 Sea of Hearts A 849, B 1973, C 1914, D 808; **Valentine's Day,** A 812, B 1973

pp. 124–125 Botticelli A 3756, B 3736, C 3772, D 3752, E 3773, F 3719, G 3767

Glacier A 842, B 1967, C 857, D 892, E 904, F 1942, G 1914